STAGES OF IMAGINATION
WORKING DRAMATICALLY
WITH ADOLESCENTS

by

David Sloan

Published by:
The Association of Waldorf Schools of North America
3911 Bannister Road
Fair Oaks, CA 95628

Title: STAGES OF IMAGINATION
WORKING DRAMATICALLY WITH ADOLESCENTS

Author: David Sloan

Editor: David Mitchell

Proofreaders: Nancy Jane, Judy Grumstrup-Scott

ISBN # 1-888365-33-1

ACKNOWLEDGMENTS

    This book has had a very long incubation period, during twenty five years of involvement with drama and teenagers. Along the way, several people have served as beacons, even as inspirations: Francis Edmunds, founder of Emerson College—the international Waldorf teacher training center I attended in the 70's—whose profound love of Shakespeare kindled my own; Peter Menaker, a gifted speech artist, actor and colleague who died at age 30 in 1981, and whose passing left the rest of us lesser lights wondering what might have been; Roswitha Spence, master costumer, puppeteer and friend to literally thousands of far-flung Emerson graduates; Ted Pugh, founder of the Actors' Ensemble, who generously spent countless hours over a decade introducing me to Michael Chekhov's work and to how it might be employed with adolescents; David Petit, whose sense for integrating music and choreography into every play added new theatrical dimensions to my work with teenagers; John Wulsin, fellow director, co-producer of nearly 30 plays over the past 15 years, and a huge part of the "we" referred to throughout the book; along with other such gifted colleagues as costumers Jill Wolfe and Chris Marlow, musicians Karen Tallman and Bill Pernice, choreographer Stephen Kotansky, technical wizards

David Johnson and Louis de Louise; my parents, who first encouraged me to write a book on the transformative power of the arts; and my wife Christine, whose own theatrical background and two "higher senses"—her sense of humor and common sense—have been a constant source of support.

For their editorial assistance in preparing this book, I am indebted to Anna Blau, Kay Hoffman, David Mitchell, and, most especially, Martha Francis. Their keen-eyed suggestions helped to clear the cobwebs.

– David Sloan
November 2000

CONTENTS

PART THREE: PRACTICAL ASPECTS OF MOUNTING A PRODUCTION

PART ONE

INTRODUCTION

Chapter 1

Assaults on the Soul

Young people today need drama more than ever.
They are growing up in a virtual wasteland for the soul, in
an age where electronic simulation has all but supplanted
direct and vital experience. As our children shuffle from
computer to television to movie screens, a number of un-
healthy effects surface ever more insistently:

— Young people rely less and less upon their own
inner resources. It is no surprise that when larger-than-
life, colorful outer images are provided for them, children
latch onto ready-made pictures instead of creating their
own. Indeed, once exposed to these pictures, children can
never really escape from these overpowering movie-gen-
erated images, which literally *dictate what children picture
for decades* when they are asked to describe a Pocahontas or
Moses or some other Disney-created caricature. As their
reliance on external pictures deepens, their own imaginative capacities begin to shrivel.

— Children spend less and less time relating to
other human beings face-to-face. A couple of clicks on the

mouse or pushed buttons on the remote can offer a universe of solitary entertainment and diversion. Interacting with a machine is more convenient, and certainly less frustrating, than having to dicker with playmates to resolve the inevitable disagreements that arise. The computer does what you want; never has instant gratification been more possible, nor more potentially damaging.

— Young people are losing their sense of what is real and what is not, what is true and what is not. As the younger generation grows up on a steady diet of simulated games and movies and shows, the line between illusion and reality blurs significantly. Sitcoms are not real, but the shows filming cops in action are, right? When the news broadcasts another nightmarish outbreak of violence, and captures on film guns spitting bullets and explosions pulverizing whole buildings, is it real or not? Is a docudrama about the life of John F. Kennedy, Joan of Arc, or Oscar Wilde true, or has it been "embroidered" to add color or controversy? Swimming in the murky waters of simulated uncertainties, young people can no longer trust their perceptions. Worse, they can grow up without moral bearings, adrift in a relativistic universe that offers only "what's true for you."

From As You Like It –
10th grade production

Drama as an Antidote

Drama work is also based on a kind of illusion, but one of the premises of this book is that the make-believe world of drama can offer a potent antidote to the soul-sapping tendencies of our age. First and foremost, it requires activating one's imagination. Despite the damage that artificially induced images can cause, young people still retain a deep reservoir of imaginative powers. They are not yet so far removed from the fertile years of childhood when creative play was a way of life, when a backyard boulder could become a pirate ship, a stick could transform into a sorcerer's wand, and a climbing tree into a fortress tower instantaneously. While they never again experience quite the same un-self-conscious delight and imaginative nimbleness as those early years, young people can reawaken such slumbering or benumbed impulses with surprising ease through drama.

Drama is also inherently collaborative, the most social of all arts. At the elementary or high school level, mounting a dramatic production demands the ingenuity and artistic efforts of dozens of people. Because all activities, offstage and on, must support a seamless vision of a theatrical totality, the process requires constant interaction between actors and directors and among the actors themselves. In our productions, the actors undertake almost all technical work, so they simply cannot work in isolation. If they try to, they learn quickly that it does not work. Two students in charge of sets for *The Skin of Our Teeth* went off on their own to build flats. Not only did they come back with set pieces that bore little relation to the overall scheme of the play, but they had also constructed them so large that the students could not fit the flats through the door of the theater! Needless to say, the smaller-scale, rebuilt sets were the result of clearer communication and cooperation.

Working on a play in this way becomes not just an artistic endeavor but a social training in community building as well. The overbearing, upstaging "star" who also wants to direct every scene and needs a healthy dose of humility, the timid actor with a small role who needs to recognize and appreciate her essential contribution to the whole, the bitterest of rivals in real life who must learn to put aside their animosity onstage and act like lifelong friends—all must face their weaknesses in the crucible of the theater. All must learn the value of submerging their own personal wishes and vanities, of working with others to create a meaningful theatrical experience.

Finally, there are the truths that can be discovered through the illusion of drama. Yet another premise of this book is that drama has the revelatory possibilities of poetry, which Ralph Waldo Emerson claims "comes closer to vital truth than history." But how can truth arise out of illusion?

Consider two different scenes that depend upon simulation. In the first, a young boy sits alone, in front of a computer, the pale light generated by the flickering images playing over his face. He is oblivious to the world outside his room, to the gathering clouds, to the rising wind, to his own dog barking because the dog has knocked over the water bowl. The boy's whole world has contracted into this screen; he sits there mesmerized, concentrating on the attacking warships, zeroes in on the video enemy, and with a clatter of keys, blasts another weapon-toting alien into cyber oblivion.

Now consider a girl onstage in a small theater, playing the part of Emily Webb in Thornton Wilder's *Our Town*. She sits on a stool, sips an imaginary strawberry ice cream soda on an imaginary counter in an imaginary soda shop. She sits next to George, her somewhat bumbling but earnest nextdoor neighbor who is about to become her sweetheart. He says,

> Listen, Emily I think that once you've found a
> person you're very fond of . . . .

10

I mean a person who's fond of you, too . . .
Well, I think that's just as important as col-
lege is, and even more so. That's what I think.

Emily replies, I think it's awfully important,
too.

George: Emily . . .

Emily: Y-Yes, George?

George: Emily, if I do improve and make a big
change . . . would you be . . . I mean . . .
could you be . . .

Emily: I . . . am now; I always have been.
(p. 94)

Like the boy sitting before the computer, this pair is
also mesmerized, but by each other; they are moony-eyed
and transported by the moment. They find themselves
magnetically drawn together. They lean towards one another, their lips almost brushing, when George bails out
and, to cover his desire and embarrassment, blurts out, "So
I guess this is an important talk we've been having." They
both turn away in awe, transformed by the enormity of
their mutual disclosures. Emily says simply, "Yes . . . yes."
The video game may entertain, but it demands
very little of the boy at the computer besides his reflexes.
By contrast, the *Our Town* scene requires of audience and
actors alike so much more of what is the core of being
human. Nearly everything in the scene is left to the imagination. The stage is bare except for two stools—no glitzy
special effects, perhaps not even any mood-setting music.
The two actors, as well as the audience, must rely upon
their own resources to make the scene real. Yet somehow, if

the actors are skilled, the girl and boy playing Emily and George can create an indelible impression, a "true" moment, recognizable to any person who remembers the first flush of young love.

The vitalizing power of imagination, the collaborative nature of the theater, the striving to portray truth onstage—these aspects of dramatic work can all counteract the adverse effects of an age that seems to value the digital over the human and the simulated over the actual. The whole process of taking some words on a page and turning them into living language, into colorful characters, into moments of real illumination, is akin to artistic alchemy. At its core, drama is an incarnating experience, just as the gradual unfolding of individuality in childhood and adolescence is an incarnating process. If, as teachers and parents, it is our highest task to help our students and children become themselves in the fullest and healthiest possible manner, drama can be one of our most dynamic means of assisting with this unfolding.

Chapter 11

Finding Meaning in
the Roots of Drama

Young people want to act for myriad reasons. In their search for themselves, most teenagers act much of the time anyway, trying on a new persona today, inventing a new walk, a new hairstyle or a new laugh for themselves tomorrow; they pose in front of mirrors and in front of their friends; they fashion an image that either completely cloaks or brashly reveals their inner selves. Drama simply legitimizes this exploration. They love becoming someone else, escaping, however temporarily, the adolescent angst that plagues so many of them. They love the intensity of working in the charged atmosphere of a play production. Many young actors discover the deep pleasure and power of moving an audience to laughter or tears. And, of course, they revel in the recognition they receive when the play ends. However, herein lies one of the inherent pitfalls for actors of all ages. Too often students are lured into a play by the promise of becoming a star, of turning into a kind of instant celebrity, an experience which they hope will catapult them towards Broadway or Hollywood.

My colleagues and I share a different approach; at every stage in our work, we stress ensemble playing over any star system, and substance over superficial effect. We want our students to understand that drama has always had its roots in far deeper soil than most of us realize. One of the first courses we introduce to high school students is *The Story of Drama*, sometimes also entitled *Comedy and Tragedy*. Exploring the Greek wellsprings of formal Western theater, students begin to recognize that drama was not originally mere spectacle or entertainment. On the contrary, the theater arose directly out of the loftiest spiritual aspirations of the Greek people. In addition to the better-known academies established to educate young boys in subjects from geometry to gymnastics, more occult mystery schools also existed in Greece, dedicated to preserving and imparting the wisdom of the gods. Two gods represented nearly diametrically opposite approaches to this search for divine wisdom. Apollo, god of light, reason, healing, and moderation, inspired a school whose disciples looked out into nature to find enlightenment. By observing as dispassionately as possible the seasons, the motions of the heavens, the cycles in nature, they apprehended those eternal laws that were the window into spiritual realities. The Apollonians' credo might be summed up in the phrase: "Nothing in excess."

The other mystery center owed its methods to Dionysus, whose name meant the "god within," who was the god not only of the vine but also of passion, inspiration, and dreams. His devotees looked not out into nature but inward into human nature—they plumbed their own inner depths to find divine wisdom. Their leading watchword, later made famous by Socrates, was "Know thyself." Followers of Dionysus would honor his life and death by drinking to excess, engaging in frenzied, orgiastic dances, and sacrificing goats, whose blood and flesh they often consumed. (Except for the animal sacrifice, high schoolers have wryly noted certain parallels between their own weekend social gatherings and these Dionysian rites).

These ritual celebrations evolved into festivals with performers and audiences. At a certain point, the narratives sung by large choruses took a revolutionary leap when one of the performers stepped out of the chorus and began to speak as an individual actor, or hypocrite. Traditionally, this moment is said to have occurred in 534 B.C., and Thespis is credited with the inspiration of creating the first dialogue with the chorus. Within a generation, Aeschylus had added a second actor, reduced the chorus, and ushered in the Golden Age of Greek drama, later elaborated by Sophocles and Euripides. It is interesting to note that at the performance of one of Aeschylus' plays, the priests in attendance became so convinced that Aeschylus had revealed some closely guarded mystery wisdom, that they threatened to kill him on the spot. Only after a desperate Aeschylus ran for refuge to the altar of Dionysus and persuaded the priests that he was neither an initiate nor an intentional betrayer of the mysteries did he escape with his life. Such an episode certainly underscores how closely intertwined early drama and spiritual seeking were.

Aristotle pointed to yet another parallel. In his *Poetics*, he wrote that the goal of any worthy tragedy was to arouse *eleos* and *phobos* in the audience, that is, compassion and awe, to achieve a catharsis of those emotions. Interestingly, in the Dionysian school, the great danger of too much inward looking was that you could suffer from self-indulgent egotism and become a slave to your passions. In the Apollonian school, the danger was that by directing all your attention to the outer world, you might be overcome by a great fear that you would lose a sense of yourself standing before the vastness of the universe. If the Dionysian neophytes could balance their selfish desires and passions with a greater awareness of others, they might develop *eleos—com-passion*. And if the Apollonian novices managed to transform the fear of losing themselves into a "fear-less beholding," they might experience the *phobos*, or *awe*, to which Aristotle referred.

Looked at in this light, every performance of a tragedy was a kind of "mini-initiation," both for actors and audience, providing them with a powerful cathartic experience designed to help them find a kind of soul equilibrium. The features of this experience seem remarkably similar to the preconditions for admission into the mystery schools, which required a purification of one's baser emotions prior to any serious spiritual advancement. Perhaps drama in ancient Greece possessed a far more sacred aspect than most people imagine.

Looking for Lawfulness

Once introduced to this background, our young actors may appreciate the loftier intentions to which drama can still aspire. We may be twenty-five centuries removed from our theatrical roots, but drama still exerts an almost primal fascination for theater and movie lovers the world over. We want to be moved, to feel deeply, to be reminded of some long-forgotten truth, or to discover some new truth through the enacted story. Our aim, in all the drama work we do with young people, is to infuse every exercise, every rehearsal, every performance with as much meaning as possible.

At the same time, we try never to forget that drama is playing, that for teenagers acting can be a form of self-discovery, as well as the successor to the imaginative play of childhood. That is why so much of our play preparation involves games and improvisational exercises designed to heighten our students' sheer delight in employing their imaginations. Following is a description of the approach to working dramatically with teenagers that my colleagues and I have developed over the past two decades. We have borrowed heavily from the invaluable resources of Viola Spolin, Peter Bridgmont, Keith Johnstone, and many others, but most of all, from Michael Chekhov, who, in turn, based his methods on Rudolf Steiner's insights into the human being. Just after World War I, Steiner designed an educational model founded upon the idea that every child is a spiritual being whose primary capacities of thinking, feeling, and willing unfold developmentally. Steiner indicated that at every stage of growth, this threefold nature needs to be nourished by age-appropriate material.

From Much Ado About Nothing – *10th grade production*

Waldorf schools have arisen in response to this need for a schooling that would primarily cultivate the will in the pre-school years, the feeling life during the elementary grades, and the new conceptual thinking that emerges at puberty during the high school years. However, because of the interweaving character of these three primary forces in every human being in every stage of life, one could say that Waldorf education was holistic long before it became a fashionable idea in educational circles. One of the great tragedies of mainstream education today is the tendency to see students as the recipients of intellectual training only. The result has been a "head-heavy" curriculum that gives short shrift to the all-important feeling realm that both nourishes and is nourished by artistic activities—dancing, singing, painting, sculpting, writing poetry, and of course, acting.

What has always appealed to me about Steiner's approach to education is his resolute insistence that our lives do not transpire randomly, in some haphazard, helter-skelter fashion. Rather, just as there is an immutable order to the laws governing nature, so there is a lawfulness to human development. Furthermore, the Waldorf curriculum is another expression of that lawfulness, if indeed at every stage of human growth, it really does respond to the needs of each incarnating child.

For some reason, the sensible sequence and order of the Waldorf curriculum eluded us when we began our dramatic work many years ago. In the midst of a play production, in particular, we directed our charges as if we were unseasoned sailors caught in a surprise squall, shouting in vain to be heard above the storm, lurching around the deck looking for secure footing, groping blindly to chart a course through the murk. It always seemed like a small miracle that the boat did not capsize and that the play (usually) survived the chaos and the commotion.

After a number of such experiences—observing the tension and strain in the cast, the occasionally berserk behavior of the directors, the way the production encroached upon the rest of the school day, the mounting pressure on everyone as the performance dates neared—we began to wonder if all this chaos was the healthiest way of preparing for a play. Couldn't we find a way of working with drama that might eliminate some of the tension-producing chaos, that instead might proceed according to the same kind of "lawfulness" as other aspects of the Waldorf curriculum?

Years of bungling and failed experiments have eventually led to the ideas described in this book. It is less a fixed system than an evolving approach to working dramatically with young people. Our approach is based upon two premises:

1) Teenagers might become better actors and more socially aware individuals by experiencing age-appropriate, sequential dramatic exercises.

2) One might use a "developmental" approach to an entire production.

To many people who have worked in the theater, this latter suggestion might seem like a patently obvious statement. You cannot jump into dress rehearsals before the costumes are designed and sewn, nor can you ask students to deepen their portrayals before introducing the characters to the actors in some way. You cannot refine the timing of entrances and exits before blocking the play. But beyond the self-evident, commonly understood stages of a production, we have developed a series of warm-ups, exercises and rehearsal methods that we believe encourage the organic metamorphosis of any play. Furthermore, this approach has helped in our striving after a balance between journey and destination. We teachers/directors should never lose sight of the performance as a worthy, ultimate goal, but we also want the process to help young actors find new dimensions in themselves. At the same time, we hope that the dramatic experience strengthens the all-important social fabric so critical to community building in our time.

Chapter III

Seeing the Whole

Working with young actors during a production requires that four theatrical challenges be surmounted:

1) Blocking—designing and "ensouling" a physical space that is both visually interesting and sup ports the characters' interactions;
2) Timing—refining the timing to such a degree that, despite varying tempos from scene to scene, a cohesive, seamless quality to the action onstage results;
3) Atmosphere—devising appropriate "atmo- spheres" that permeate and intensify every scene, providing an invisible, unifying substance that charges the entire play;
4) Characterization—creating believable characters whose conflicts, failings, dreams, and triumphs touch the audience.

None of these critical undertakings should be at- tempted before everyone involved first understands, then envisions, the *totality* of the play. In preparation for our productions, we spend some weeks with our students care- fully reading through the text of the play aloud. We try to identify central themes and movements of the play. On a practical level, one of the great preliminary challenges of any production is to translate an overarching vision of the play into an artistic, visually arresting poster. Students work long hours trying to design some central image that somehow captures the essence of the play. For *Twelfth Night*, one student used black and white to great effect by creating interlocking, silhouetted mirror images to represent the theme of twins in the play. Another student drew an old jalopy overloaded with people, pots, and bedding as the centerpiece of a *Grapes of Wrath* poster.

This activity of trying to comprehend the totality of a play is not simply an intellectual exercise; it also has applications far beyond the practical. Michael Chekhov advised actors to "fly over" the whole of a play in their imaginations, so that they carried onstage at the beginning of the first scene a picture of the last moments of the final scene. Why? Acting is as much a way of conveying invisibilities—unexpressed intentions, dimly felt urges, secret desires—as it is of expressing the tangible and concrete. If thoughts can be considered realities, then possessing such an all-encompassing vision of the play may actually help bring coherence and unity to a performance.

It is a sign of the complex, fragmented times we live in that fewer and fewer people seem interested in or capable of seeing the totality of a situation. In their naturally self-absorbed and preoccupied way, teenagers are especially prone to missing "the big picture." We work hard at helping our students appreciate the design, the movement, the underlying aims of the play. Such an approach gives young actors practice in acquiring that broader perspective so lacking in modern life.

Only when our young actors have begun to see the play as a colorful and living tapestry do we begin to incorporate the other key elements required of a successful production that were mentioned above: blocking, characterization, timing, and atmosphere. But in what order should they be tackled? Attempting to work with all aspects of staging simultaneously had previously yielded only chaos and way too much pressure. For some clear direction, we decided to return to the very basis of Waldorf education, that is, Steiner's understanding of the growing human being. It seemed to us that a play's incarnation might parallel in some fruitful ways the incarnation process of the very students we were directing.

Conquering Gravity

During the first two or three years of life, children primarily come to know the world *spatially*. Even infants will flail their limbs in a seemingly random fashion, before they discover they can flip themselves over and raise themselves up on their arms in preparation for crawling. Children may develop at somewhat different tempos, but the phases they pass through provide a common time sequence for us all. Some children begin crawling at six months, some later, but nearly all will crawl before they stand, and stand before they take those first miraculous steps, and walk before they talk. Their whole existence seems dedicated to conquering gravity and exploring the physical space surrounding them. They are in constant movement when they are awake, learning the textures and shapes of things, and albeit more slowly, the distances between them. I will never forget the sight of my then two-year-old son, now nearly two decades ago, standing before the sliding glass door in the kitchen one crisp winter evening, mesmerized by the silver splendor of the full moon. After a long moment, he stretched his arm up and out toward the moon, trying to scoop it up in his fingers. Undaunted by his first failure, he tried again before dropping his arm and being content to admire the moon from afar. Such moments, and countless others, teach us about our spatial limitations as well as our possibilities.

Taking our cue from this seemingly inherent human desire to orient ourselves in space first and foremost, we ground virtually all of our drama work by beginning with movement and gesture exercises. Shakespeare was speaking of poets when he wrote that they "give to airy nothing a local habitation and a name," but he could just as easily have been referring to directors. In terms of a play, the blocking—the rough skeleton of entrances and exits, general playing areas, the spatial relationships of characters—provides a similar anchor for young actors. They may not know who they are yet, but they begin to get comfortable with where they are.

Yet the *who* cannot be ignored; after all, bringing characters to life is the foundation of all drama. Simply shifting students around the stage without their having any sense of *how* their characters move is like trying to play chess without understanding the directional possibilities of the pieces. So early on, our young actors become acquainted with their characters' gestures, their gaits, their physical idiosyncrasies. Later, as students get to know their characters, they will dig into interior spaces—fears, wishes, motives, the why of character development—which will add depth and dimension to their portrayals. Indeed, this is one of our actors' most significant challenges. They will need to focus their energies on character development from the very beginning to the very end of any production. (Chapter IX, entitled "Finding Each Other: Ensemble Playing" explores this element in more detail.)

The Pulse of the Play

Only after the actors develop a strong sense of the space of the play and of their characters' movement through that space do we attempt to refine the element of time, or timing. It is far more difficult than the blocking to orchestrate, as any director of a farce will confirm, and it can only really be precisely calibrated once the physical "map" of the play has been designed. On the great space/time continuum that circumscribes our lives, we conquer space long before we make any sense of time. Tell a five-year old that she should come in for supper in ten minutes; if you don't intervene, she may well continue blowing dandelion fluff into the wind until dark. Or tell her that there are only three more hours in the car until we reach grandma's house, and see how many times in the next hour she asks, "Are we there yet?" At around age six or seven, children begin to acquire some bodily grasp of time, mainly through rhythmic games—playing hopscotch, jumping rope, skipping—which is soon followed by a more conscious relationship to time. Third graders in the Waldorf school learn to tell time; nine-year-olds also begin to see the larger sweep of time, looking back on their younger years with comments such as, "When I was a kid, I sure was cute." They may also begin to look to the future with real longing or even apprehension. The first faint recognition of their own mortality can whisper to them at this time.

This same visceral understanding of time that children possess becomes a tool in the theater for exploring a character's tempo. Does he move through the world dragging his heels or bouncing along at double time? Does she have the mercurial metabolism of a sparrow or the sluggish digestion of an ox? Does she breathe slowly and securely or shallowly and anxiously? Does he speak ponderously or with a "machine gun tongue"?

This question of breathing can be expanded to consider how a particular scene, or even how the entire play, "breathes." Shakespeare, of course, is the master of varying the pace within his plays. The inspired insertion of the gravedigger's black humor just before the climactic final scene of *Hamlet* allows the audience a much needed "exhalation." If a play is well paced, it can actually deepen the collective breathing of an audience. Conversely, a poorly timed production—one in which breathless actors rush through lines in scenes that career into one another like bumper cars—can almost suffocate an audience, leaving actors and spectators alike feeling cramped and unsatisfied.

So the time structure of a play can imprint itself as surely as the space in which it is enacted. In fact, one might

24

say that the rhythms within a play sculpt the space within a play. Who can remain unaffected by the compelling pace of the "Get thee to a nunnery" scene between Hamlet and Ophelia? It begins deliberately, with an almost tender greeting; then, fueled by Hamlet's suspicion that Ophelia is "bait" dangled by her father to determine the source of Hamlet's "madness," the scene lurches out of control. It accelerates with all the speed and unforeseeable force of a train derailment, as Hamlet's whirling words leave Ophelia crushed and bewildered. Such variations of tempo can leave the audience with an afterimage as palpable as the tracks left on asphalt by squealing, smoking tires.

Charging the Atmosphere

In any absorbing dramatic piece, actors create an atmosphere onstage, permeating the scene with a kind of electrical charge that augments the mood. Before they are teenagers, children have less ability to understand or to implement this idea of suffusing the air around them. That is one reason most early elementary school productions, no matter how artfully staged, lack depth and dimension. This capacity to really charge the atmosphere only comes with the onset of adolescence. The miraculous transformation from child to teenager is not just another small step up a smooth marble staircase. The two stages of life resemble one another in the way a candle flame resembles a forest fire. Looking at a contented, clear-eyed, well-proportioned ten-year old, who could foresee the dramatic outer and the turbulent inner changes that would make that same child nearly unrecognizable four or five years later? Much is made of adolescents' becoming sexually mature, of their biological ability to conceive children, even though they are just out of childhood themselves. But what of their newfound capacity to conceive abstract ideas, to think more conceptually than ever before? And what about the rich and strange new interior world they begin to plumb? Children seem content to skim along the surface of the water;

adolescents long to dive beneath the surface and discover a wondrous world below, full of shadowy shapes, dark caverns, darting color.

As teenagers begin to experience the deepening of their own burgeoning inner lives and the accompanying, unpredictable storms of their mood swings, they also acquire the possibility of recreating those storms onstage. Many years ago I directed seventh graders in a production of *The Miracle Worker*. It had been a difficult class to teach, a mob of rude and unruly hooligans at their worst, a spirited but resistant group even at their best. Tackling a play with the emotional resonance of *The Miracle Worker* was extremely risky, but somehow they managed to harness their otherwise seething energies. The two girls who portrayed Helen Keller and Annie Sullivan were particularly gifted, as was evidenced best in the dining room scene where the young girl playing Helen acted like the spoiled child of darkness she had been brought up to be—groping her way around the table during the meal, using her fingers to help herself to anyone's plateful of food, discarding what she did not want on the floor. When Annie could no longer bear to sit another moment witnessing this display of unbridled crudeness, she insisted that the rest of the family leave the room so that she might begin to teach Helen some basic dining etiquette. What ensued is one of the greatest battles of will ever conceived for the stage. Annie threw down the gauntlet by physically picking up Helen, pushing her down in a chair, pressing a napkin in her lap, and forcing her to eat with a fork. Defiant to the end, Helen kicked, bit, and flailed away, trying in vain to escape this determined, strong-armed stranger.

The irony of such a seemingly violent scene is that it can only be played by actors who have a great deal of self-control. The two young girls in these roles had to precisely calibrate their movements to avoid seriously injuring each other. At the same time, they had the challenge of expressing all the rage and single-minded tenacity they could summon. To help them in this regard, they worked on saturating the scene with an atmosphere of bristling tension. Although they were only thirteen at the time, these two young teenagers relied on their own quickening imaginations and newfound emotional depths to create a scene of passionate intensity.

Getting Some Size

Twenty years ago, a dear actor friend of mine once heard me complaining about some trifling problem. He chided me for being so self-absorbed, declared that it was beneath me to get enmeshed in such pettiness, and exhorted me to "get some size." I have forgotten what the problem was, but I have never forgotten his advice; indeed, I regularly pass his wise counsel on to my young players. We enlarge our characters and get some size for ourselves when we extend our awareness beyond our own self-imposed limits to the possibilities that arise in interaction with others.

Earlier, I mentioned character-building as the most central and ongoing challenge of any production. During each of the other stages—orienting the players in space, developing a sense of tempo, and creating an objective mood—actors strive to become convincing characters. As in real life, however, this incarnation process may be the most difficult undertaking of all, for it comes closest to the core of what it means to be human. People search for this mysterious "self" all their lives; some expect to find it walking well-lit avenues; others plunge down forbidding, unmarked trails. How can teenagers, who are not fully ego beings yet, hope to discover the essential self of the characters they must play?

They find it in the same way female authors describe male characters so insightfully, the way younger playwrights enter so knowingly into the psyche of the old. They use their powers of observation and, above all, their boundless capacities of imagination. Surely Walt Whitman touched upon a universal truth when he proclaimed in his *Song of Myself*, "I am large, I contain multitudes." (p. 74) We all contain male and female: the long-suffering and the robust, the faint-hearted and the bold, the bumbling and the graceful. They simply need to be recognized and liberated. The imagination unlocks all doors, makes accessible all remote and uncharted regions of the soul.

We use dozens of different imaginative exercises to help our young actors become acquainted with these many sides of themselves. Some involve closed-eye visualization as the basis of character-building. We ask students literally to put their characters on, as they would pull a nightgown down over their heads. They picture the way their characters stand or sit in a particular scene, the way they speak a line in that stance, the gestures they employ. With their eyes still closed, the students outwardly strike their character's pose, then come to life, simultaneously speaking their lines aloud to the accompaniment of the gestures they have visualized. They work improvisationally with their characters as six-year-olds, as ninety-six-year olds; they compose love letters to their characters' sweethearts, and they speak at their own funerals.

An Alternative Method

This imaginative approach to developing character offers students an alternative to the most influential current acting technique, popularly known as "the Method." One of the Method's primary tenets is that actors can rely on their own reservoir of feelings to uncover the requisite emotion they might need to play a particular scene. If they need to express anger onstage, they find some situation in their past when a parent or friend provoked rage in them. Once the feeling is identified and reawakened, the actors learn ways of harnessing and transferring this emotional recall to the present acting moment. This approach sounds appealing, because actors need look no further than their own personal experiences to stoke the fires of their craft. In the twentieth century some of the world's greatest performers have used the Method to create an often imitated realistic style.

But is this technique appropriate for teenagers? I have my doubts on several grounds. I wonder if adolescents have developed the necessary objectivity to be able to distinguish between the real emotion experienced in the past and the "reheated" feeling now employed for artistic purposes. It is a hard enough distinction even for adults who are accomplished performers. I heard about an actress who played Lady Macbeth with a touring company. Over the course of several weeks she had to play this demanding role—one of the most ruthless and malevolent females ever seen on the stage—eight times a week. Halfway through the tour, she had to be replaced because she had used the Method to such an extent that she could no longer separate her self from that of Lady Macbeth; she became possessed in a way. The dark and depraved side of herself, which she uncovered to play the role, took complete control of her private, as well as her professional, life. The actress could no longer escape her own creation.

To avoid such entanglements, the imaginative approach described above is less invasive and offers a built-in safeguard. Any role that can be put on as externally as one puts on a costume can also be taken off just as easily. I am always amazed that our students can be very much themselves as they get into costume and makeup just minutes before a performance, then go onstage and become a raging Leontes in *A Winter's Tale* or an irrepressibly loony Madwoman of Chaillot with astonishing conviction. A moment after the final curtain, they are excited, distracted, and back-to-abnormal teenagers, thinking more about the cast party than about the play they just performed. Such an approach gives young people the possibility of shedding their characters and retaining an invaluable kind of freedom in the process.

Another concern I have about employing the Method with teenagers is that instead of helping them healthily meet the world, it drives them ever more deeply into themselves. It is all too easy for any adolescent, not to mention an aspiring actor, to get stuck in his or her own subjective rut. By their very nature, adolescents tend to see the world through the filter of their own subjectivity. Indeed, Rudolf Steiner's great exhortation to teachers of adolescents was to help lead them from their own subjectivity to the objectivity of the wider world. Even without the Method, teenage actors tend to focus on their roles, their scenes, without giving much thought to that critical interaction between characters, where the drama really occurs.

During the latter part of a production, we use exercises that encourage our students to break out of the narrower confines of their own roles, to widen their world by "embracing" all the other characters in the play. They exchange lines, props, even entire roles in rehearsal. They shadow each other onstage, provide physical and verbal mirrors for one another in warm-ups. By constantly having to enter into the experience of the other, students develop a heightened awareness that takes them beyond themselves. In this respect, drama offers a creative vehicle for meeting one of the great challenges of our time—recognizing and cultivating a sense for the uniqueness of others. What is community building if not a means of honoring the individuality in every other person without losing our own sense of self?

The Final Ingredient—Add Audience and Stir

What director has not had the experience of charging frantically around for several weeks trying to whip a production into readiness, only to lament three days before the performance that, "If only I had another week, this play might not be a disaster waiting to happen!" We *never* have enough time. At a certain point, usually less than five minutes before opening curtain, the director may find a quiet corner and say a little silent prayer. He prays that some interested, guiding spirits might help keep the duct-taped set from collapsing; he implores them to keep the back of the leading lady's dress closed with a bent bobby pin because no one could find a single safety pin in the entire costume room; he humbly asks that the terrified student playing the messenger, who has never once spoken his five measly lines correctly, finally gets them right.

Then, more times than not, prayers are answered. The set does not even wobble, the dress remains intact, the messenger not only remembers his lines, he speaks with the perfect blend of authority and deference. Moreover, the actor playing Captain Cat in *Under Milkwood* suddenly sounds exactly like the old sea salt the director envisioned from the start. The characters are more animated than ever before. Characters who never acknowledged each other's presence really listen to one another. They fill pauses with real feeling. Some of the players incorporate inventive gestures that were never rehearsed. What is happening? It is as if a kind of grace has descended upon the stage.

When the final ingredient—the audience—is added to a play, magic occurs. It is impossible to prepare young actors for that electrifying feeling of opening night, when the atmosphere that the actors have been trying to fill with one emotion or another is suddenly pulsing with anticipation. Through some unexplainable alchemy, the audience helps the players to breathe new and unexpected vitality into lines that had been rehearsed dully dozens of times before. When this happens, it is as if the play assumes an existence independent of the director's efforts. For males involved in the theater, this experience is as close as they will ever get to giving birth; for females, it may be a preview of actual labor pains. This is the moment that directors hope for, more than the applause after the final curtain or the kudos of the parents or even the gratitude of the young actors, who more clearly than ever now see the fruits of all their labors. Every such birth of a play confirms over and over that there are indeed guiding spirits. Our audience may be far larger than we imagine.

From Much Ado About Nothing – *10th grade production*

PART TWO

"INCARNATING" A PLAY

Chapter IV

THE FIRST PHASE: FREEING THE PHYSICAL

If we follow in a theatrical sequence the previously described phases of human development, the first stage of production will correspond to that early period of life when children get to know the world spatially. Phase one of our play productions emphasizes the physical orientation of the actors. This orientation can work on three levels:

1) Initially, as warm-ups and games that help to stretch and loosen participants' physical organism

2) As an avenue for arranging the larger spatial relationships of the play, also known as blocking

3) As a method of exploring the physicality of their specific characters

Warm-ups

Actors need to tune their instrument as diligently as do professional musicians and singers. In the case of students, such exercises provide more than an opportunity to limber up; they act as a transition from whatever activity our students have just completed to the drama at hand.

If our young actors drag themselves into class as if all the blood has been drained from their bodies, we turn to exercises that wake them up. Conversely, if students come bouncing in like bowling pins, other warm-ups can focus their energy, help slow them down, even dissipate some of the inner tension they often carry.

Warm-ups activities should be used at the beginning of classes or rehearsals. Because of chronic time constraints, the temptation to forego such exercises and leapfrog into the middle of rehearsal is often overwhelming. However, taking such a shortcut would be tantamount to eating a potato raw. Our students could probably swallow it without it killing them, but later on they might complain of indigestion. Warm-ups and games help young actors to prepare for the short run—the rehearsal at hand—and for the long run as well, by introducing some of the basic skills underlying dramatic work—concentration, adaptability, peripheral awareness, presence of mind, playfulness.

Most of the exercises described below are best done in a circle. It is the form that best reinforces the ensemble idea; everyone is in the same relationship to each other and equidistant from a center. There is no front or rear, no place to hide, no obvious leader or follower. What happens within a circle has a binding, unifying quality, as several of the exercises underscore.

Exercise 1: YES

One person begins by making eye contact with someone across the circle and gazes at the other individual until the person receiving the gaze says, "Yes." The first person then crosses toward the second person's spot in the circle. However, as the first person moves, the second person must link eyes with a third person, who, in turn, must say, "Yes." Then the second person moves towards the third's place, while the third person makes eye contact with a fourth, and so on. This exercise should begin slowly. Once the group becomes accomplished at the sequence, it can be played silently, with people simply nodding their heads instead of saying "Yes." This is an excellent focusing, calming activity.

Exercise 2: BALL TOSS
     Have one person in the circle hold a bean bag or tennis ball. This person again makes eye contact with someone else, then calls out that person's name before tossing the ball, *underhanded and very deliberately*, to the recipient. The idea here is to underscore the importance of the tosser making real contact with the recipient of the toss. On a simple but metaphorical level, this activity parallels the give-and-take so essential to dynamic theater.
     A more challenging variation of this exercise is to have two balls being tossed around the circle simultaneously. Another is to turn the circle of people into a "walking wheel," whereby the tosser attempts to throw to a moving target.

The next few warm-ups involve passing something around the circumference of the circle, sometimes for the sake of speed, sometimes for precision.

Exercise 3: PULSE
     Everyone in the circle holds hands. Someone begins by squeezing the hand of the person next to her, who follows suit by squeezing the hand of his neighbor. The objective is to pass the pulse around the circle as rapidly as possible. Two variations: 1) Try passing the pulse with eyes closed. It will probably travel faster! 2) With advanced groups, try passing a pulse both clockwise and counterclockwise simultaneously, but be forewarned—it gets very confusing.

Exercise 4: PASS A STRETCH
     One person in the circle performs some stretch or limbering movement— for example, rolling t

bending at the waist and touching toes. The person to the left or right then does the same stretch and adds another. The next player reproduces the first two and adds a third. The object here is not only to loosen up, but to be so observant that each person imitates the preceding movements as precisely as possible.

Exercise 5:   PASS A FACE
Someone begins by making a ridiculous face, with or without the help of fingers to distort one's features. Then the student turns to a neighbor and holds the expression while the neighbor mirrors the face as accurately as possible and then passes it along. This is also a good exercise in self-control, because the whole idea of passing around some absurd facial expression is sure to elicit laughter.

Exercise 6: PASS A SOUND
This is one of many vocal warm-ups that aid actors in loosening up their mouths, throats, and breathing, all critical tools of the trade. Start by uttering a consonant or vowel, turning toward the person next to you as you vocalize a "Shhhhhhhh" or a "K" or an "Aaaaaaah," expelling as much breath as possible in the process.   In quick succession the sound is passed from one player to another. You can alter the sound from consonant to vowel or vice versa when it completes the circle. You can also send one sound in one direction and another in the opposite direction.

Exercise 7: SINGING TO THE BLIND
Another vocal warm-up, which also requires intensified listening capacities, begins by pairing people up. One person volunteers to be blind, simply by closing her eyes. The other participant stands *behind* his partner and begins to sing or hum some tune. It can be anything, from some recognizable piece with lyrics to some purely improvised humming. Whatever the singer chooses, he then moves

slowly backwards or sideways, but always close enough for his partner to hear. As sailors were drawn inexorably towards the haunting sounds of the legendary sirens' in Homer's *Odyssey*, so the blind participant follows her partner's singing. However, not wishing to cause the shipwreck awaiting the Greeks, the singer must protect his blind partner from crashing into any other students by leading her safely around a room full of other moving pairs.

Exercise 8: PASS A CLAP

As with other movements around the circle, this begins with one person clapping once and having each successive person follow with a single clap as rapidly as possible, creating an "applause wave."

Exercise 9: PASSING HOPS

Imagine this time that a mouse is scuttling under everyone's feet in the circle. One person starts the motion by hopping on one foot, then the other, in quick succession. The next person does the same, to make way for the invisible, racing rodent. Anticipation is the key to this exercise.

Exercise 10: PASS AN IMAGINARY OBJECT

This is really a miming exercise, which calls for vivid visualization and the precision of a surgeon. Begin by creating out of thin air, with your hands, some familiar object—say, an umbrella. You must fashion the umbrella very deliberately, from the curved wooden handle to the button that opens the top. Creating such objects involves intense concentration and commitment; they will only be as real as one's imagination conceives them and one's hands coax them into being. Even imaginary objects need to have weight, texture, clear boundaries, dimension, even color!

Once the umbrella is "visible," hand it to the person next to you, who acknowledges it, perhaps by shaking rain off it before collapsing it. Then beginning with the umbrella, the student transforms it into another object. He uses magic hands to elongate or crush or hollow out a new article out of the old. After reshaping the umbrella into, say, a yo-yo, he does a trick or two and passes it on to the next person.

For a hyperactive class, this is a remarkably absorbing, settling activity. Students will delight each other with their imaginative creations and ingenious transformations. Where else can mops turn into frogs and rakes into suitcases except in the dextrous hands of inventive young people?

Exercise 11: CLENCH AND UNCLENCH

We do this exercise standing, but it might be even more effective if students are lying on their backs. Begin with the toes; have participants tighten all the muscles in their feet for a count of perhaps five, hold their breath as well, and then release it. Move up to the calves—clench for a few seconds, hold breath, then release. Do the same for each major muscle group as you move up the body, with particular attention to the shoulders and neck. This can be an effective way to settle a rambunctious class or to end a tension-filled rehearsal.

Exercise 12: FINDING ONE'S BALANCE

Students should stand as upright as possible, with their feet together, and fix their gaze on a distant point. Have them shift their weight as far forward as they can without moving their feet or losing their balance. They should hold this forward position for several seconds. Then have them lean back as far as they can, again without losing their balance. Finally, lead them back to a balanced midpoint between the two extremes. Here they can appreciate the stability that comes of establishing an equilibrium.

Exercise 13: BECOMING A MAST

Another relaxation exercise is to have participants close their eyes and imagine that their bodies are masts on a ship. Have them place their feet together and, without bending at the waist, sway back and forth to the movement of the waters gently rocking the ship. The waters could also become stormier, which would have the consequence of forcing the masts to roll and reel more vigorously, even to the very verge of their balance points.

Exercise 14: HAND WRESTLING

For this exercise, students should pair up, without regard for relative height or weight, and face each other. Have them place their palms, fingers up, against their partners'. Then, in silence, each pair should have a "conversation" with their hands by pushing into one another, creating some resistance and, simultaneously, exploring the space between them. First one person should take the initiative and lead, then the other. Then, neither student should take the initiative—rather, together the pair tries to "sense" which direction their hands want to move, without imposing anyone's will. Finally, and this is a very difficult next step, you might ask students to do this exercise without touching palms at all, but rather mirroring each other's movement. (See MIRRORS, Exercise 26.)

Students need to be forewarned that this is not a competition or one of those games designed to see who can knock the other off balance. Rather, the intention here is to develop a sensitivity to the unspoken impulses that can weave between actors if they "listen" attentively enough with their palms.

Exercise 15: DYING A THOUSAND DEATHS

Ask each student to imagine a melodramatic, silly, or ingenious way to die. Then have each one enact his or her demise, either simultaneously or, far more preferably, in succession. Some memorable mimed deaths have included: swallowing a toothbrush; parachute failure leading to a "pancake" end; getting flattened by the barbells one actor had lifted above his head; electrocution induced by picking up a downed power line. Have them act out agonizingly long death-throes, during which someone feigned being stabbed and, not unlike Pyramus' absurdly prolonged expiration in the play within the play in *A Midsummer Night's Dream*, they flop around like a fish on the floor for several minutes, appearing to die a number of times before resuscitating long enough to moan and convulse yet again.

Exercise 16: CIRCLE MIRROR
One participant makes a random movement (do not let anyone think too long before moving), with an accompanying vocal expression. Someone might flap his arms as he bounces on the balls of his feet and shouts "Wheeeeeeop!" As soon as he completes the gesture, the entire circle in unison mimics the movement and sound as precisely as possible.

Games
Games are rarely played solely for their diversionary value. Each of the following games demands participation that helps cultivate fundamental dramatic capacities. What are those basic skills? Most games require heightened social awareness, an intensified sensitivity to what's happening outside oneself; others necessitate quick thinking and lightning reflexes, presence of mind, grace under pressure; still others ask students to develop an inner flexibility. Such games really become a training to enhance the inner mobility actors must rely on to respond to any unexpected current during a performance.

Exercise 17: GOTCHA

One person stands in the middle of the circle and calls out someone's name. The person whose name is called must instantly drop to the floor, while the person on either side turns and points to the other, saying "Gotcha." Slow reflexes are a liability here. If the original person whose name is called does not duck quickly enough to avoid being in the line of fire of one of his neighbors, then he becomes "it" and replaces the player in the middle. If he ducks quickly enough, then the slower of the two neighbors pointing and calling out "gotcha" will go into the middle. The player who was in the middle takes the place on the circle of the person who replaces him or her. This game is wonderful for a group needing to familiarize itself quickly with its members' names. Even for a group well known to one another, the exercise stimulates alertness, energy, and tremendous concentration.

Exercise 18: ZIP/ZAP/ZOP

Like GOTCHA, this game requires the reflexes and the peripheral awareness of a hummingbird. All the members of the circle press their flat palms together and hold them, fingers pointing up, in front of their chests. One player starts by pointing her "hand sandwich," fingers first, at someone across the circle, saying, "Zip." The person being pointed at must then either aim directly back at the first player or at another person on the circle and say, "Zap." Without missing a beat, the third person must either return the aim to the Zapper or to yet another player, saying "Zop." The idea here is to make sure that the "Zip, Zap, Zop, Zip, Zap, Zop" sequence is followed in order and with increasing speed as the students become proficient at the game. Any member of the circle who either fails to respond to being someone's target, or who says one of the "Z" words out of order, is out of the game and must become a active spectator. The idea here is to increase the speed of the exchange until it is a rapid-fire showdown between two or three survivors.

Exercise 19: CHANGING PARTNERS

A large space is most desirable for this very active game. Participants stand in pairs, arms linked, around the circle. A chaser is designated, as well as a chasee, who tries to avoid being tagged by the chaser. The chasee can find a safe harbor by linking arms with any person standing in a pair. Once this occurs, however, the person on the other side of the newly formed trio must release to become the chaser, and the chaser abruptly becomes the chasee. This is a frenetic game, full of mad pursuit and sudden reversals. No physical activity is better for demanding the presence of mind needed to instantaneously shift from pursuer to pursued.

Exercise 20: SOURCE OF THE MOTION

Viola Spolin included this among hundreds of dynamic exercises in her definitive book *Improvisation for the Theater*. Students sit in a circle, except for one volunteer who leaves the room while a leader is selected. This leader begins some rhythmic movement—tapping, clapping, nodding, or the like—which everyone else imitates as exactly as possible. Then the volunteer re-enters the room, goes to the center of the circle, and attempts to identify the source of the motion. All the while, a crafty leader will slightly alter the movement; the other participants will immediately adapt to the change, without looking directly at the leader, of course. If the volunteer correctly guesses who started the motion, the person who was the source now becomes the next volunteer to leave the room.

Exercise 21: STREETS AND ALLEYS, or CAT AND MOUSE

Students stand in a number of straight rows, at least four to six, comprising of four to six people each. Rows should be equidistant from one another, no more than an arms' length apart. Participants create "streets" by joining hands with students in front of and behind them. They create "alleys" by dropping hands with their street partners and joining hands now with students standing in rows to the left and right of them. Two other students have been held out of the row formation; one becomes the cat, the other, the mouse. The cat begins at one end of a street, the mouse at the other. The cat will, of course, chase the mouse and attempt to catch it by tagging it. However, students will instantly switch from street to alley formation when the teacher calls out, "Switch!" What was a clear avenue for the cat suddenly becomes a stone wall, created by students' bodies. The cat cannot go over or under any such walls, but must instead follow only the open streets and alleys created by the students' shifting arm positions. The teacher should call switches often and unpredictably.

Exercise 22: HA-HA AND HEE-HEE

Arrange the group so they are sitting in circle, with you among them. Have in your hands two common objects, such as a pen and a tennis ball or a book and a fork, and designate one as a "ha-ha," the other one a "hee-hee." (You could call them anything you like—I've most recently used two nonsense words—a "spobo" and a "peelee".) Then turn to the person on your left, hand over one of the items, and say, "I give to you a ha-ha." Since everyone in the circle suddenly has no memory, the person asks, "A what?" To which you reiterate, "A ha-ha." Then that person turns to the next participant and says, "I give to you a ha-ha." The third person, in turn, asks "A what?" Now the second person has already forgotten what the object is called and must turn back to you to ask again, "A what?" Again, you reply, "A ha-ha." The second person then turns back the third person and passes along the information, "A ha-ha." After the object has passed through several people's hands, the communication begins to echo and re-echo around the circle: "I give to you a ha-ha." "A what?" "A what?" "A what?" "A what?" "A what?" "A ha-ha." "A ha-ha." "A ha-ha." "A ha-ha." "A ha-ha."

As confusing as this may sound, the real confusion begins when you pass the other object in the other direction. Now there is a "ha-ha" moving clockwise, and a "hee-hee" proceeding counter-clockwise around the circle. What happens when these "ha-ha" and "hee-hee" chains meet and must pass each other? With "A what?" "A what?" coming from both directions and needing to be passed on to neighbors on both sides, the potential for pandemonium is enormous. However, many groups manage to successfully pass both items around the circle and back to the teacher, albeit not without a number of false starts, dead ends, and a great deal of laughter.

Exercise 23: HAGOO

This game comes from the now-classic *New Games* book first published over twenty years ago, which spawned a whole generation of creative, noncompetitive activities. This one is perfectly suited for teenagers who need to develop self-control onstage. One of the most undermining situations that can occur at this theatrical level is when an actor drops out of character and smiles at an inappropriate moment. Hagoo helps to counter this tendency in young, inexperienced actors. Participants divide into two lines, facing each other, far enough apart to create an aisle. Then one person slowly begins to walk down the aisle, looking at everyone she passes, left and right. The aim of the people forming the aisle is to make the walker laugh. They may make ridiculous faces, speak in cartoon voices, tell a joke, catcall, mime some characteristic gesture or phrase of the walker, fling a (tasteful) insult, anything short of physically touching the walker. No tickling, pushing, poking, or intimidating allowed! If the person passes through the aisle without cracking a smile, she is congratulated and takes her place at the end of the line. If she fails, it is back to the beginning for another go-round. Then another student at the head of the line attempts to be a stalwart stoneface as he walks the gauntlet.

Exercise 24: BALL FREEZE

As in the warm-up BALL TOSS (Exercise 2), both the tosser and intended receiver in this exercise must heighten their awareness of each other, or they may literally and figuratively drop the ball. Both must focus on what passes between them—in this case, the ball—for a successful "communication."

A much more challenging version of the ball toss is to set people in motion around the room. Instead of walking in a circle, students go wherever they like. However, everyone's focus must be on the person with the ball. The instant the ball is caught, everyone freezes until the person in possession of the ball decides to move again. A still more intensified version of this exercise is to transform the ball into the world's most precious and fragile object. Now when the tosser throws the ball, everyone darts toward the intended receiver, surrounds him, and becomes a human cushion, to prevent a bobbled toss from hitting the floor. Again, the instant the ball is caught, everyone freezes.

This game does wonders for teaching attentiveness to that all-important central focus of any theatrical moment. It also requires the tosser to become ever more aware of his or her body language. It is all too easy to suddenly and unpredictably toss the ball to an unsuspecting receiver. The real challenge of the game is to develop a strong sense of intentionality, so that one's fellow actors can begin to "read" with confidence one's movements.

Chapter V

Blocking

The term blocking does not describe the process of developing a spatial map of the play; it implies a series of rigid, cumbersome, unalterable decisions. Indeed, it can be a tedious, dispiriting activity. Some directors meticulously chart in advance, on paper, every cross, every gesture their actors should make in every scene. Then they shift the students around the stage like chess pieces. The result can be deadly, with young actors moving rather mechanically along prescribed paths onstage without a clue about what impels their characters to do so.

This initial blocking work can be much more fluid and dynamic. Of course, directors need to envision the general movements within and between scenes. But the director who thinks he can precisely map out the play's blocking, in its unalterable totality, even before the first rehearsal, is probably kidding himself. Entrances and exits have to change as set pieces appear. Crossings left and right, up and downstage, should evolve more out of characters' deepening interactions than out of some abstract scheme. In fact, deliberately making minor changes in the blocking periodically may actually keep the actors fresh and flexible.

Taking a show on the road makes such changes inevitable. Several years ago our sophomore class decided to share their production of *The Merry Wives of Windsor* with a number of schools in the Northeast. The first school we visited had a most unwelcoming, awkward space at one end of a small gymnasium. Unlike our own modified arena stage, with exits leading out through the audience that surrounds half the stage, this stage was very deep, half as wide, and cut off completely from the audience. Needless to say, we had to alter virtually our entire blocking in one afternoon rehearsal. After our five-hour bus ride, I knew that probably half of what we had changed would be utterly forgotten by supper. Yet that evening's performance was one of the cast's most animated. It was both nerve-wracking and breathtaking to witness the students improvise their movements on the stage and adjust to each other's ingenious staging. In one scene, a confused actor entered from the left, exactly opposite the direction from which the actress onstage had just turned and called. When he made his unexpected entrance from behind her, the character already onstage swung her head around and ad libbed, "Oh, there you are! I'm all turned about!" Somehow she had the presence of mind to stay in character, and at the same time, artfully cover his mistake. The appreciative audience never knew they were watching largely improvised action during the entire play. Had our original blocking been more rigid, I'm not sure the actors would have been so adaptable.

On another occasion, three days before our first performance of *The Mouse That Roared*, one of the leads broke his leg skiing. We had no understudies, so rather than cancel the play, we decided to have the professor play his part in a wheelchair. We had to make emergency adjustments with the blocking, including adding a ramp, but again, the changes seemed to enhance, rather than diminish, the performance. I was particularly struck by how much more verbally expressive the young actor with the broken leg became when he could no longer rely on his body language.

Stage space almost always means an unnatural space. Players become weary soldiers on a battlefield, sprites in a forest, enraged demonstrators in the streets, lawyers arguing in a courtroom, lovers on a moonlit beach, all in an artificially designed, extremely limited acting area. Most stages provide only a frontal perspective. If performers adhere to the old theatrical maxim, "Never turn your back on the audience," they are forced to contort themselves in contrived and almost painful positions—bodies facing forward, heads twisted sideways. How can we create situations onstage that appear to represent more natural movements, while still honoring the constraints of such limited playing areas?

Teachers/directors need to familiarize themselves with some basic laws about moving around in a stage space. These certainly don't apply to all stages; arena staging, for example, which has audience either partially or completely surrounding the playing area, requires special consideration of how to orient various scenes. Actors will always be cutting off some portion of the audience to offer another section unobstructed views. But for most stages, the following points may be helpful:

1) Different levels onstage usually offer more visually arresting scenes than action which takes place on one uniform level. Platforms, ramps, ladders, balconies, crates, spiral staircases, tree stumps—dozens of imaginative set pieces can provide possibilities for varied elevations. In the absence of such set pieces, actors onstage can at least vary their relative heights by sitting, standing, or squatting to offer more interesting groupings.

2) Young and inexperienced actors tend to stand too close to one another when speaking onstage. Perhaps they assume that the same distances between people apply whether they are onstage or not. But when we transfer

our typically intimate, conversational proximity to the stage, the actors seem jammed together, with too much empty, dead space around them. Unless the actors are either engaged in some conspiratorial scheme or a romantic interlude, putting more space between actors than in ordinary conversation creates more interest and even more tension.

3) In general, inexperienced actors need to enlarge their movements and gestures onstage. One of my mentors explained it in the following manner: Imagine putting a life-sized statue, mounted on a pedestal, in a closet. In that small space, the statue will appear enormous. However, if you put that same life-sized statue in the middle of a stage in a theater, the statue will suddenly appear quite small, dwarfed by the space surrounding it. Therefore, those of us who are life-sized actors need to become larger than life onstage, or we, too, will actually appear smaller than life!

This point was driven home to me when my wife and I went to a performance of *Kiss of the Spider Woman* on Broadway. In the most compelling scene in the play, Chita Rivera, in the lead role, appeared in black at the center of an immense, light-created web. At that moment, she seemed to expand beyond the limits of her own body, to fill the entire stage with an intensified energy, presence, aura. After the play, we were fortunate enough to go backstage and meet Chita Rivera. We were astonished when we encountered a very petite actress instead of the giantess she had become in the web. She had certainly learned how to "get some size" onstage.

4) Certain situations seem to invite archetypal movements by the actors. For instance, when some secret needs to be revealed, some aside spoken, some intimate moment shared, actors invariably move downstage, closer

to the audience. When one actor wants to show that she's in control of a situation, that she's got the upper hand over another character, she can move in an slow arc behind that character while both are facing the audience. An upstage position tends to confer, or at least indicate, power or knowledge. Characters wishing to spy on others most often conceal themselves upstage. Think only of the famous garden scene in *Twelfth Night*, when Malvolio unsuspectingly reads aloud the forged love letter in front of a (barely) concealed Sir Toby Belch and friends.

5) Creating friezes at critical moments in a play—that is, freezing the actors in various positions—can be both visually arresting and awakening for both audience and actors. Such "living snapshots" are very difficult to hold for very long, but they can disclose what otherwise might be missed in normally paced action. One overused but still effective method would be to freeze all other figures in a scene while one character makes a pointed aside to the audience.

At the end of the second act in the play *The Skin of Our Teeth*, by Thornton Wilder, a deluge of Biblical proportions is heading towards Atlantic City. In the descending darkness and whirling winds, the Antrobus family is frantically dashing around the boardwalk trying to locate one another so that they can board an ark before the pier collapses. Just as the mother screams out the real name of her missing son Henry—"CAIN!"—the action freezes. For a moment, all that breathless, frenzied movement is held in check, and the audience can behold each family member in some revealing pose. Then Henry/Cain appears, the only figure onstage moving, which accentuates his isolation from the rest of his family. Within a heartbeat, the action resumes at breakneck speed towards its Noah-esque conclusion. Artfully composed freezes can leave indelible impressions with an audience.

6) Young actors need to learn how to enter *before* they actually enter, to exit *beyond* the actual stage exit. The tendency is to begin to act just as they cross that invisible threshold dividing onstage from off. However, the most effective actor will begin acting thirty seconds before he hits the stage. That way his entrance will be a convincing continuation of what was already begun in the wings, instead of some rather jolting transition from his street self to his onstage character.

7) Crowd scenes are among the most difficult to block. Most groups congregrate onstage to support and focus the central action. However, they can be static, deadly displays, especially if the group exudes all the interest and energy of grazing cattle. As in real life, most members of an onstage crowd feel a certain anonymity and an accompanying lack of responsibility for taking a dynamic role in the scene's success. In terms of blocking, the worst two extremes include either:

a) stringing a group out in a straight line, the "police line-up" formation, or

b) clumping everyone together into a hydra-headed mass, within which certain actors can completely hide from the audience. Smaller, spread-out groupings within the larger crowd often create more interest, with each member of these subgroups related on some level to those nearby. Ideally, each player also conveys some individual quality, without distracting from the main interaction onstage.

The real key to staging potent crowd scenes depends upon the ability of the group to be true beholders, to be such active listeners that they act as funnels to focus the audience's attention on the central action. At the climax of

The Winter's Tale, Leontes and his court go to see the unveiling of a statue of his supposedly long-dead wife, Hermione. When she stirs, then comes to life, the members of the court in the background recoil as Leontes recoils; they gasp as he gasps, gape in amazement and finally witness one of the most touching reunions in all of Shakespeare's plays. Without the court members there to reinforce Leontes' (and the audience's) reactions, the scene loses part of its heart.

8) Every actor onstage needs to move from one spot to another with some purpose in mind, impelled by the inner demands of the character or situation. Too often directors have their players move from one spot to another in a scene simply to create an opening on the stage for another character's entrance. Following such mechanical directions is worse than painting by the numbers, because onstage the journey is every bit as important as the destination. The conviction with which a character moves will ultimately determine whether the movement works or not. Consider the lovers in *A Midsummer Night's Dream*. Demetrius, who has been hotly pursued by the hateful Helen across the stage, may suddenly turn on her and advance menancingly. He does this not just for the sake of variety but out of desperation—fleeing the tenacious young lady does not seem to be working , so he changes his strategy and says,

> You do impeach your modesty too much
> To leave the city, and commit yourself
> Into the hands of one that loves you not:
> To trust the opportunity of night,
> And the ill counsel of a desert place
> With the rich worth of your virginity.
> > (Act II, scene ii)

On a mundane level, it seems most sensible to block the play chronologically and as quickly as possible. We have found that a week's worth of hour-plus rehearsals is usually enough to get through a slimmed down version of a full-length play. Students need to bring pencils and scripts to these classes and to be prepared to erase and revise initial blocking directions. They must also become familiar with the actor's stage orientation. Very few of them know that stage left or stage right is the actor's left or right as she faces the audience. Fewer still know that upstage means the area furthest away from the audience, and downstage the closest to the audience. They need to understand what it means to upstage a fellow actor. If they saw a production with a raked, or inclined stage, it would become instantly clear. On a raked stage, suppose I stand somewhat behind other actors. Not only am I then higher, and appear to have more stature than my fellow actors; I also force them to turn away from the audience in order to address me. The spotlight is on me! It is all too easy for young actors to unwittingly upstage other players. Sometimes, of course, it is fitting to have every other character onstage focusing the audience's attention on a figure upstage. But this should be done consciously and not by happenstance.

Chapter VI

Grounding the Character

In our everyday lives, we constantly express our soul moods through our physical natures. If a teacher is edgy and irritable, students may notice immediately that his gait becomes more clipped in the halls, his head tilts forward in a battering ram mode, his gestures sharpen. How students sit in a class often betrays the level of tension or comfort they feel. Are their legs and arms crossed protectively? Do they sit upright attentively, or do they sag in chairs apparently more subject to Jupiter's gravity than to Earth's? As teachers, we learn to "read" our students' body language. It can, of course, be a deceptive science. I recall one pupil who dominated classes with her overblown gestures and general bravado. Yet in a private conversation on a camping trip, she shared deeply about feelings of insignificance. Another student had suffered through the slow, agonizing death of his mother. His outward iciness disguised his fear of getting too close to other people whom he might lose. Yet more often than not, our body language reveals much more about ourselves than we would like. The anxiety-filled fellow drums incessantly on his desk; the angry young woman "punishes" the floor when she walks, heel-heavy; the sanguine socializer bounces on the balls of his feet and talks with quicksilver hands; the timid girl tucks her head between her shoulders, casts her eyes downward, and wrings her hands.

So it is with the characters students portray. Unlike the fictional figures in novels whose innermost thoughts and feelings can be disclosed through the author's omniscient point of view, characters onstage usually must rely on the external to communicate, i.e., the words they speak and the actions they take. Therefore, students need to learn how to be physically expressive, how to fill their movements with meaning. One of the most recognizable characteristics of inexperienced actors is the way they unconsciously use their hands to illustrate every phrase they speak. They flap, point, flail, sweep, and sever the air around them. In the process they often distract their audience more than they ever convey to them. They need to awaken to every gesture, every sidelong glance, every tilt of the head that might reveal some nuance of soul.

We begin with the simplest of exercises, which introduces students to their own physicality. We ask students to walk around the room, becoming aware of their gait, the way their feet touch the floor, the position of their toes, the stiffness or looseness of their joints, the way their arms swing, the sway of their hips and arch of their back, the tension in their shoulders, and the angle of their chin. Students usually experience a good deal of self-conscious discomfort at first, especially if some of the participants sit out and become an audience. I would recommend as a general principle the idea of involving all actors at the same time in these early exercises, both to maximize participation and to reduce performance anxiety.

After becoming familiar with their own natural gait, students participate in a series of exercises devised to break their habitual movement patterns, to introduce a new plasticity" and heightened awareness into their gestures.

Exercise 25: FOLLOW THE LEADER

Sometimes the simplest of children's games can help develop valuable capacities. Divide the class into a number of small groups, perhaps four to six members per group. A leader is randomly chosen for each group, with the rest of the students falling in line behind him or her. The leaders then begin moving around the room, independent of the other lines, in their own inventive ways, with the followers behind each leader attempting to imitate as precisely as possible the leader's movements. It helps if the leaders move slowly, rhythmically, and rather predictably. At a given signal from you, the leader moves to the back of the line, and the next student in line assumes the leader's role until all members have had an opportunity to lead the line.

Exercise 26: MIRRORS

Pair students up and position them to face one another, an arms' length apart. Have one of the actors in each pair raise his or her hand, thereby designating that person as the initiator. The initiating students should imagine themselves standing in front of a full-length mirror. Instruct them to begin any slow deliberate movement, so slow, in fact, that the other student can easily and simultaneously copy the gesture. The objective here is for each initiator and mirror to move in such a synchronized fashion that an observer would not be able to distinguish between who was beginning the motion and who was following.

In the beginning students will probably limit their movements to hand gestures as they explore the plane between them and their mirror. However, one can encourage full body involvement. Have them imagine the costume their characters might wear, from stockings to sashes, from footwear to jewelry, from hoop skirts to hard hats. Then ask students to put their characters' outfit on in front of their mirror, finishing perhaps with a characteristic pose or two.

Another variation of this exercise, related to PASS A FACE (Exercise 2), is to have the initiator make some grotesque face in front of his or her mirror, the kind people make when they first get up in the morning and inspect for example, their teeth, tongues, complexion, and barely visible moustaches. Of course, in all these mirroring exercises, students should exchange roles and partners as the director sees fit.

Demonstration of Exercise #26

Exercise 27: ENVIRONMENTS—THE FOUR ELEMENTS
Since imagination is our most potent ally in working with young actors, we ask them to picture themselves moving (and then to actually move!) over varied terrain and in unusual situations. The possibilities here are endless, but here are a few tried and true favorites:
First have students imagine they have been caught in a *clay avalanche*; they are buried but still standing. The

clay is soft enough for them to push away, but not easily; it offers resistance and the pushing requires hard work. Their goal is to gradually push enough clay away from their bodies so that they have room to move. They might start by using an elbow or knee or nose or finger to nudge back a bit of the clay, until they gain enough space to use their hands to create a "clay-free zone" completely around themselves. This should be done slowly, silently, and laboriously, with a great sense of exertion.

As a follow-up and antidote to the clay work, fill the room with imaginary water, so that the class can experience the *underwater*, slow-motion delights of floating, swaying like kelp, feeling the buoyancy and lightness bearing them ever upward. To really appreciate this imaginative environment, normally quick-moving students constantly need to be reminded to hold back. Under water, there can be no sharp or sudden movements. The element slows and softens every abrupt gesture, rounds out every straight line. If the actors do this well, the whole room will turn into an eerily silent, slow-motion, aquatic dance.

Next, the students head for the sky. Have them become leaves or clouds or scarves fluttering in the breeze. They cannot help but spin, flutter, and twirl their way around the room, barely touching the floor. Again the students need to feel the levity of the air, the freedom of flying, unencumbered by gravity. The only caution here is that mid-air collisions can occur if people are not acutely aware of their air-borne fellow travelers.

The element of *fire* can be introduced in one of two ways, depending upon one's aim. To stimulate dynamic movement, have participants imagine the floor transformed into hot coals; students will instantaneously begin to bound about, hopping from one hot foot to another. The energy level will soar in the room, as will the noise level. To offer students a quieter experience of fire, have them close their eyes and imagine a candle or torch, steadily burning within them, in the region of their chest. Students should walk around the room feeling themselves the source of infinite warmth and light. You will know whether they are really inwardly experiencing this radiating quality if students begin to stand more upright and slow their pace as they walk around the room sharing their light. This is a tremendously effective exercise for any young actor whose character needs to develop the warmth and generosity required of a noble soul.

These explorations of the four elements can offer more than just an experience of earth, water, air, and fire. They may also serve as outward expressions of four fundamental character types. Widely accepted in the Middle Ages, the concept of the four temperaments was revived by Rudolf Steiner to help educators develop deeper understandings of their students. For actors as well, these general types can be useful, as long as they realize that people are never purely one temperament or another. Each temperament possesses its own strengths, as well as posing its own set of challenges.

The *choleric* is often associated with the element of fire. Energetic, ambitious, even driven, the choleric individual is nothing if not intense. If he or she can control this inner fire, the choleric person can grow into a motivational leader, a trailblazer who initiates dynamic activities. The choleric who does not learn to master the bursts of anger to which he or she is very vulnerable can turn into the unpredictable volcano, whose eruptions leave a wide swath of destruction.

The *sanguine* character is a creature of the air. Mercurial, gregarious, often irrepressibly cheerful, a predominantly sanguine person will have a wide range of interests and a natural desire to pursue them all at the same time. Sanguines typically are jacks-of-all-trades—in their most evolved form, a Leonardo da Vinci or a Thomas Jefferson. In class, sanguines are the students whose attention flits from the blackboard to their neighbor's lunchbag to the ball game being played on the field outside the window. They are exceedingly awake in their senses and have an impressive peripheral consciousness; they can tell you what everyone else in the room is doing. I have long relied on my now-teenage daughter's sanguine awareness. Because she notices everything, she has always had an uncanny knack of knowing where I absent-mindedly left my glasses or car keys or briefcase. The danger here, of course, is that sanguines can lose focus all too easily and have trouble regaining it long enough to complete the task at hand.

People with *melancholic* dispositions are fairly easy to identify. They experience life more inwardly, and often more painfully, than either cholerics or sanguines. They tend to be highly sensitive souls, sometimes hypersensitive, whose more refined sensibilities often lead them into artistic fields. They can feel the ever-present tension between inner desires and outer demands, between the noblest ideals and the harshest realities. The fictional Faust expressed the melancholic's deeply felt lament.

> Two souls, alas, are dwelling within my breast,
> And one is striving to forsake its brother.
> Unto the world in grossly loving zest,
> With clinging tendrils, one adheres;
> The other rises forcibly in quest
> Of rarefied ancestral spheres.
>
> (p. 145)

Their element is the earth, which they carry either as a great burden or as a plastic, transformative substance.

Individuals with *phlegmatic* tendencies initially appear quite sleepy, or at least dreamy. Their inner clock operates more slowly than the choleric's or the sanguine's; they need more time to eat and digest, their schoolwork as well as their food. And yet, given the time, they can absorb an experience more deeply than the extroverted types.

Phegmatics draw little attention to themselves, will sit quietly in the midst of an uproar, as if transported to some other realm. For that very reason, they are the best people to turn to in emergencies. Their watery nature, their placid, unruffled demeanor, can stem hysteria in a frightened child or rising panic in a roomful of people. Phlegmatics can be therapeutic personalities if they overcome a tendency toward passivity and inner lethargy.

I remember long ago hearing a description that used the simple act of throwing a ball to distinguish these temperaments. A sage Waldorf educator of many decades' teaching experience said that if you throw a ball to a choleric, she may pick it up and hurl it back to you twice as hard. If a sanguine catches the ball, he might bounce it a few times, toss it behind his back and spin it on his finger before throwing it to someone else. If you throw a ball to a melancholic, she might respond in a victimized tone, by saying, "Why did you throw that ball at me?" And the phlegmatic might say, after the fact, "What ball?"

How can young actors use temperaments in their characterizations? Keeping in mind that these predispositions are really more qualities than types, consider the typical gait of each temperament. Cholerics tend to stride purposefully, fast-paced, hard on their heels; sanguines contact the earth more lightly, bouncing on the balls of their feet. Melancholics may walk tentatively, thoughtfully, perhaps almost reluctantly, while phlegmatics take their time; they amble more than stride over the ground. Choleric gestures might be sharply defined, energetic, aggressive, even explosive. Sanguines' hands will flit and flutter nimbly, while the melancholic may gesticulate almost melodramatically to accentuate some overwhelming feeling of angst. Phlegmatics tend to move their limbs very little if they do not have to. Such impressions are by no means to be considered definitive descriptions, but they can serve as broad indicators from which students can construct believable characters.

Exercise 28: WAYS OF WALKING

Have students slog through an imaginary *swamp*, the water first up to their ankles, then their knees, then their waists. While we require silence for most of these exercises, for the swamp walk, we encourage our students to make their own sloshing, sucking, and slurping sounds.

Put them on an imaginary *tightrope or highwire*, fifty feet off the ground, and have them slowly make their way from one side to the other. A horizontal balancing pole is optional. At a certain point, you can have them do this exercise as if in a high wind, or somewhat intoxicated, so that they teeter, reel, wobble, but never completely lose their balance. Under no circumstances should they fall off. One other variation involves students beginning to feel quite confident on their wire and asking them to perform some amazing trick—a leap or spin or some other "sleight of foot feat"—that will leave audiences far below gasping in awe as the highwire artists land expertly back on their perch.

Other ways of walking are limited only by one's imagination. Here are a few suggestions. Have participants walk as if they:

- — have on concrete shoes
- — have springs on the balls of their feet
- — have someone sinister following them
- — are cowboys
- — are robots
- — are runway models (Surprisingly, the boys usually have no problem with this one if all participants look foolish simultaneously.)
- — are monsters or giants
- — are elves
- — are clowns wearing oversized, floppy shoes
- — are five years old (Encourage them to interact with this one. Out of nowhere skipping, playing hopscotch, jumping rope, sandbox

playing, teasing, crying, block-building, and block-knocking-over will appear. The energy level of the room will soar.)
— are ninety-five years old
— are taking their first steps as toddlers
— are carrying the world's most precious Ming vase
— are grotesquely obese
— are the center of attention
— have arms with a mind of their own
— have no bones in their bodies

Exercise 29: STICK/BALL/VEIL/CANDLE

Have students close their eyes and, using their hands, create in front of them an imaginary stick of some kind. Then have them open their eyes and begin to move about the room with their sticks, leaning on them as if they were canes, waving them about like swords, twirling or tapping them. Young people often have a tendency to talk during these activities. While there will be a time for such verbal interaction, side chatter while moving disperses focus. Unless otherwise indicated, silent attentiveness is the general rule during these initial exercises. As they explore the space with their sticks, very gradually the sticks disappear and become internalized; the actors no longer carry sticks—they become sticks. Every movement they make now has a stick-like character. While each student's interpretation of this quality may vary, most of them begin to walk much more rigidly and woodenly around the room. Their gait will slow, joints will stiffen, and gestures will become much more angular.

Next have them freeze, then drop out of their stick character. Again, have students close their eyes, this time imagining a rather large beachball. Again have them open their eyes and move around the room, playing with their beachballs—bouncing them, batting them in the air, showing their dimensions and positions through their hands.

After playing for a brief time, the gradual transformation occurs in which the external objects vanish and the actors become beachballs. Their movements now lose all angularity; they bounce or waddle or bob as curves triumph over straight lines.

The same sequence holds for the next two objects. With the veil, the internalization should lead to leaping, rippling, whirling, and spinning around the room, as if the students were some veil or scarf fluttering in the wind. Their movements with the lit candle (or torch, if a larger scale is desired) will be much more deliberate. At first, students need to walk slowly enough to tend to their "flame," but as they internalize the light you should see the same kind of radiating quality described in the fire section of the FOUR ELEMENTS exercise.

Such an exercise provides more than imaginative fodder for young actors; it may also introduce them to new and surprising dimensions of their characters. For example, in *A Midsummer Night's Dream*, Egeus, Hermia's unyielding father who demands that she marry the man of his choice or else, could be played with a good deal of stick-like intractability. The actor playing the hot-headed Demetrius could incorporate an inner blazing fire, while Titania's fairies might move with airy spriteliness. In each case, young actors incorporate these qualities in three stages:

1) imagining and playing with the external object,

2) internalizing the object so that the actors become the thing itself,

3) refining and distilling the inner experience of the object so that what remains is an essence that adds intriguing undercurrents that vitalize their characters.

Exercise 30: CENTERS

One of Michael Chekhov's most effective techniques for developing character involved the exploration of centers. According to this idea, every character—for that matter, every person—operates from a particular center of energy. This is not some mystical force, such as an Indian chakra. Rather, these centers are really the creation of one's imagination and heightened awareness of a very specific physical area of the body. For example, imagine putting a character's center in an eyebrow. How will that center be expressed in gesture and movement? It is often a revelation to watch a roomful of teenagers suddenly raise an eyebrow in supercilious fashion, tilt their heads up so as to look down their noses at the rest of humanity, and begin to walk around the room in the most condescending manner.

Simply by directing their attention to a specific region of their bodies, young actors can often find a key that unlocks part of a character's nature. Have students place their center in their knuckles, and watch their hands ball up into fists as they begin to pace pugnaciously around the room. Or ask students to locate their center just above their heads; several actors have used this idea to become characters who are either air-headed or inebriated.

The location of the center is not the only variable that actors can employ. They can also play with the substance of the center itself. Imagining a red-hot center, like a glowing coal, will elicit a very different response from that of a center that resembles the sharp end of a stalagmite. As an illustration, students might imagine a center that is like a hard little ball placed at the very end of their noses. How will this affect their movement? The vast majority of participants will thrust their heads forward and bustle about the room pecking and poking their noses into other people's space in the most meddlesome and intrusive manner. For a character with an inquisitive or nosy disposition, such a center would be perfect.

By contrast, if students were to relocate their center to their lower abdomen, and turn it into a soft, squishy, jello-like substance, their gait might slow to an amble or a stroll; were they to engage each other in conversation, their speech might edge into a southern drawl. Such a center has the tendency to give people a sense of well-being, almost lethargically so.

These characterizations are not theoretical—I have observed dozens of different groups of young people engage in these exercises, presumably with few preconceptions about how one center or another would affect their movements. Allowing for individual variations, it was nevertheless striking to see how many students moved in similar ways when exploring one center or another. Is there some objective truth behind these experiences that we can use in the theater?

Michael Chekhov believed that just as an emotion might lead to an outer gesture (e.g., a feeling of anger might be outwardly expressed by making a fist), conversely some outer gesture might also evoke an inner response. Most of our work with centers has verified this contention. Sometimes we will ask students to simply make a fist, without attaching any preconceived emotional content to the gesture, and then play an improvised scene. Inevitably, the actors' interaction will move towards some belligerent confrontation. If we ask them to begin a scene using the gesture of reaching their arms toward one another, usually some sympathetic exchange will take place, some reconciliation or comfort achieved.

Exercise 31: CLOSED EYES

Without a doubt, this exercise serves as the cornerstone of all our character-building work with students. Virtually every other dramatic exploration they undertake during a production flows from this inner activity. In fact, we believe so fervently in the power of this imagination that we ask young actors to do closed-eye exercises daily in preparation for a play. Furthermore, we have come to the realization that if audiences experience any uncommon vitality and conviction in our actors, this single exercise may be one of the primary reasons for our students' success.

Have students stand in a relaxed manner, eyes closed, with some space around them to move. They should imagine their characters at some particular moment in the play. Beginning with the feet, they need to build as detailed a picture of the characters as possible, led by the director's guiding questions:

Physical Inventory

1) How do their characters stand? Do their feet rest on the ground firmly or tentatively? Does their weight rest evenly or tend more to the inside or outside of their feet? When they walk, do their feet hit the ground heel-first, toes-first, or balls-of-feet first? Are their feet pigeon-toed or splayed at all?

2) How do their legs feel? Do they have young or old limbs? Do they experience any stiffness in the knees? Do their legs feel like springs or pistons, or are they filled with lead? Are their arms long or short for their body? Do they swing freely when the characters walk, or are they tightly held by the sides? Are their hands rough and calloused from outdoor work? Are their fingers nimble or fumbling?

3) How about the regions of the hips and loins? Do the hips sway more than usual when the characters walk? Is the sphincter tight or relaxed? When the characters walk, do they lead with their loins?

4) How do the abdominal areas feel? Are the digestive processes too active, constantly rumbling, or do the characters feel a sense of well-being? Are they overweight and flabby in the middle, trim and fit, or too thin, even scrawny?

5) How do they breathe? Slowly and deeply, or rapidly and shallowly? Are they smokers who breathe raggedly and raspily? Or are they so well-conditioned that they seem tireless when they run? Are they ever aware of their heartbeat? Does it beat strongly and rhythmically all the time, or does it flutter irregularly?

6) What do they "carry" on their backs and shoulders? Do they stand squarely upright, or do they stoop? Do they suffer from chronic lower-back pain or tightness in their shoulders? Can they touch their toes when they bend over?

7) How much tension do they feel in their necks? Can they easily turn their heads, or is there a restrictive stiffness there? Do they feel their necks to be long, elevating the heads well above their bodies, or are the necks so squat that their heads seem to sit nearly on the shoulders?

8) What do their countenances reveal? Do they have thin, pursed lips, a broad forehead, a sallow complexion, a pug-nose? Do they gaze steadily or blink nervously, always glancing sidelong at the world? Do they have a thick, unruly haystack of hair or thinning wisps combed over from the side?

After repeated efforts to experience this physical inventory, students will begin to become acquainted with their characters. They may object— "How do I know what her joints feel like? I've never been a 38-year-old pregnant shopkeeper!" As always, the director simply encourages such young actors to place their faith in their inexhaustible imaginations.

Visualizing the Costume

Now ask your students, still with closed eyes, to picture the clothing their characters might wear, beginning with undergarments. This exercise will usually be used long before the actors will have their actual costumes, so their imaginations can have free rein. Have them visualize every last detail of their entire outfit, from footwear to headgear. Are their characters barefoot, wearing lace-up boots, expensive Italian shoes, smelly old sneakers? Do they have on tight skirts or baggy pants, loud Hawaiian shirts or slinky silk blouses, burlap tunics or kings' brocaded robes? Do they sport bowlers, helmets with visors, diadems, fedoras, flowered straw hats? What accessories might complete their characters' attire—pocket watches, scarves, pearl necklaces, swords, spectacles, goatees?

Throughout this guided costume tour students should be directed to pay special attention to the colors and textures of the fabrics, as well as to their characters' overall appearances. Are they generally slovenly or fastidiously neat? Do their clothes fit them well, or do they look like a sausage in outfits two sizes too small? Do their shoes pinch? Do their hats continuously fall over their eyes? To make this exercise more outwardly active, you can instruct your students to actually mime putting on each item of clothing as they inwardly picture their apparel.

Vitalizing Every Moment

These closed-eye activities can be taken much further, enlivening virtually every scene in which the actors are involved. Have them choose a particular moment in the play when their characters have a line. They need to picture as precisely as possible the physical position of their characters at that moment. Are they standing disdainfully, with hands on hips, glaring down their noses at an unworthy subject? Are they sitting hunched over and weeping at the news they have just heard? Are they about to embrace their lovers? Whatever the stance, ask your students to actually place themselves in that position, not vaguely or tentatively, but definitely and sharply. Now, still using their imaginations, they need to hear their characters say the line accompanying those poses. Then, on a given count, have all of the actors open their eyes and simultaneously speak their lines, bringing as much energy and animation into the moment as possible. When they have all finished, have them once again close their eyes, see and hear inwardly what they have just done, and then perhaps have them repeat the whole process, only this time have them pose, speak, and move even bigger—with more volume, more intensity, more conviction. Daily repetition of this exercise—asking students to find different moments in the play which they literally imagine into being—will gradually bring each character to life. The characters will acquire a depth and dimension not typically accessible to young actors.

Exercise 32: PLAYING WITH IMAGINARY PROPS

Yet another variation of the closed-eye work is to have students picture their characters with some prop—either one scripted in the play or an object that this particular character might use. In a recent production of *Under Milkwood*, imaginary items included an umbrella, a pipe, a book, a swaddled infant, a fishing pole, a glass of ale, a shovel, a cleaver, a dog on a leash, and a vial of poison. First the actors, eyes closed, use their hands to create their objects in front of them. They need to be encouraged to create as precisely as possible, giving not only shape but also weight and texture to their prop. At a given signal, have all students open their eyes and begin to walk in character around the room, using their props as they go. After a few moments, have them pair up and stand in front of one another. In silence have them show each other what their props are by indicating their shape, weight, and purpose. Then have participants exchange props by carefully handing them over to their partners. Now, armed with new props that probably have absolutely nothing to do with their characters, have the actors continue to move about the room in character, acquainting themselves with their newly acquired objects. Again at a certain point have the students create new pairs and repeat the process of demonstrating and exchanging props. In this manner young actors learn to make imaginary objects real onstage.

Exercise 33: WALKING IN AND OUT OF CHARACTER
After some initial closed-eye work, students begin to at least picture their characters' distinctive gaits. This exercise can help them outwardly experience the difference between their own ways of walking and their characters'. Divide your rehearsal space into two clearly delineated areas. In our case, we designate for one area a series of three wide risers where our audiences usually sit. The other area is our stage, a wooden floor that the risers partially surround. Have your students begin walking normally in one area or the other; in our case, the area of the risers makes the most sense. However, the instant their feet touch the wooden floor, have the actors transform themselves into their characters. Now a free-swinging teenager becomes a twisted old crone, dragging an arthritic leg across the acting area, or a harried business man pacing brusquely back and forth, or a King's daughter striding nobly through an adoring crowd. Then, the moment they cross the dividing line between areas, have the students revert to their normal gaits once again.

Demonstration of Exercise #33

This activity will be most effective if participants imagine that the boundary between the two areas is a threshold not unlike Alice's looking glass or the back of the wardrobe in the Narnia stories. They move instantaneously from one realm to another, without warning or any transition time. In addition to helping strengthen the contrast between their own natural walks and their characters', this exercise also enhances that all-important inner mobility so critical to good acting.

Exercise 34: GETTING TO KNOW ME

Take your cast of characters on a journey into their imaginations. Have them assume their characters and mime preparing for the trip. What will they wear? Have them identify and then simultaneously speak aloud the name of the color most often worn by the character. What will they bring with them? What foods do their characters crave? Make sure they at least bring a musical instrument that most reminds them of their characters. Soon after they begin the journey (do have your actors walking around the room), their characters encounter an obstacle. What is it? How do they surmount it? Have participants actually do what they imagine their characters would do. Further on, they meet an imaginary stranger who insults them. Have them engage the stranger in a spirited exchange, but make sure the characters only respond in gibberish. After the stranger departs, instruct the characters to grow tired and to sit down by a stream to eat. Have them mime very carefully the action of unwrapping a sandwich, nibbling on some cheese, or dipping their hands in the stream to drink.

After lunch, ask the characters to take out their instruments and play them. Have the students vocalize the sounds they are making. Then have them resume their journey. Perhaps they find an object along the way that reminds them of themselves. What is it? Actors should pick the object up, make it as real and visible as possible, and then either take it with them or discard it. Finally, the characters should reach a hut and find a wise old woman inside. They will ask the woman a revealing question about themselves, such as "Why am I always angry?" or "Will I ever find true love?" or "How can I overcome my restlessness?" Perhaps they also share with the old woman their innermost fear before they depart and head home.

Such a journey can be as wide-ranging or probing as the director's inventiveness allows. The aim here is to have the students become better acquainted with their characters by exercising their own imaginations. Any journey that challenges actors to perform physical tasks in the manner of their characters and, on a deeper level, to plumb the psychological depths of their characters, will be beneficial. A more advanced version of this exercise is described in Exercise 51: CHARACTER BIOGRAPHIES.

Exercise 35: ANIMAL BLIND

This exercise is really a prologue to a most helpful character-building activity. First, have students stand randomly throughout the room and either blindfold them or simply have them close their eyes. Whisper in each participant's ear the name of an animal (those that make distinctive noises are best; fish are very hard to enact)—for example, a mouse, cow, elephant, lion, pig, monkey, seal, snake, hyena, bee, cat, horse, crow, bear, wolf, owl, porpoise. Then announce that the cast's objective is to arrange themselves in order of their animals' relative sizes. The only clues they may give each other are the characteristic sounds their animals make. No speaking allowed! (On occasion, we have had one student remain human, to see if he or she might assume a key organizational role; presumably, this person would possess the reasoning capacity to help sort out the animal order.)

Exercise 36: ANIMAL QUALITIES

Once a class has successfully completed the previous exercise, the director can deepen the actors' exploration of character by asking the students to think of an animal that reminds them of their character in some way. However, the resemblance certainly should not be restricted to the physical level. Our whole realm of soul qualities shares much in common with the animal kingdom. One only needs to look back to ancient myths and legends in virtually all cultures to confirm this notion. Many gods are depicted as having animal heads and human bodies— Anubis the jackal-headed, Horus the falcon-headed, and Thoth the ibis-headed from Egypt come to mind; so do the centaurs and minotaur from Greece, as well as the shifting animal disguises Zeus assumed in his dalliances with mortal women.

Demonstration of Exercise #36

Even our language contains vestiges of a time when the boundary between the animal and the human was much more fluid. Why else would we refer to one person as "lion hearted," another as "pig-headed"? We refer to men who prey on innocent women as "wolves," someone who acts cowardly as "chicken" or a "spineless jellyfish." A treacherous individual is called a "dirty rat" or "snake"; someone who is exhausted is "dog-tired"; an embarrassed person appears "sheepish."

Therefore, it is not so far-fetched to ask students to find animal qualities in the characters they play. We may need to offer suggestions to those participants who draw a blank in this regard. Perhaps one character has the nervous metabolism, and the darting movements of a squirrel; another, out of a painful shyness, may pull her head down towards her shoulders like a turtle or strut like a rooster or bray like a donkey when she laughs. Once they have identified some quality, we lead them through a three-phase exercise:

1) Have them all first become that animal, complete with distinctive movements and sounds. To minimize that feeling of looking foolish, which can be so incapacitating in drama, it is far better to have all cast members move as animals simultaneously. The menagerie that fills the room will then be a source of delight for all of them.

2) Next, have the actors close their eyes and imagine this animal quality being incorporated into their characters in some fairly obvious way. A gorilla-like quality might involve lengthening some actor's arms or scratching himself intermittently; a snaky character might narrow her eyes or flick her tongue suggestively; a horsey character might develop the habit of pawing the ground with his foot or snorting to punctuate his comments.

3) Finally, have the students pair up and engage each other in some improvisational conversation, now incorporating their animal mannerisms into their characters.

They may be too obvious or heavy-handed at first; it will be the director's job to help actors refine and internalize these qualities. Eventually, these cruder animal attributes may all but disappear from view, but still add an animating, energizing dimension to characters.

Exercise 37: EXAGGERATED MIRRORS

One of the students' favorite rehearsal techniques involves mirroring one another. This is a more complex variation of MIRRORING (Exercise 26), because it combines verbal, as well as physical, interaction. As with the closed-eye exercise, ask students to think of a line from the play and visualize their characters in some specific stances, using some purposeful gestures. Students should open their eyes, find partners, and one at a time, speak their line in character, complete with appropriate stance and gesture. Now the partner's task is to act like an after-the-fact-mirror; in other words, after one actor has finished speaking the line, the mirror repeats it, with the accompanying movement and gesture, but all in a wildly exaggerated fashion. An almost imperceptible nod transforms into a vigorous shake of the head, a half-hearted pointing finger becomes a piercing thrust, a weak wave is magnified into a grand sweep. A line spoken with some mistrust, "I have questions about you," becomes a shrieking, over-the-edge accusation—"I HAVE QUESTIONS ABOUT YOU!" Then the partners switch roles, with the original mirror offering a line and the other actor exaggerating every aspect of the delivery.

Students delight in this exercise—it sanctions a type of aping and parodying so common to teenagers. However, because it involves mirrors lampooning characters, and not people mocking the people creating those characters, the mimicry can occur without any hint of a personal attack. The exercise is also very freeing; students who have, up to this point, played it safe, or who have remained wooden and inexpressive, can suddenly become animated clowns.

Directors should be forewarned—this exercise will raise the energy level of a group to such a degree that it may be difficult to reel the students back in, unless you use a time-tested technique which we refer to as

THE FREEZE

This is less an exercise than a method of curbing the sometimes unbridled enthusiasm exhibited by teenagers. One of the mixed blessings of doing drama is that, in their exploration of character, young people can momentarily lose themselves, or at least lose their sense of appropriate restraint. We have found that The Freeze counteracts students' tendency to spin too far away from their centers. The Freeze works very simply. During any exercise or activity, the director says (or screams—sometimes the noise level requires more volume) "Freeze!" whereupon the participants stop dead in their tracks; no matter what the position, they become statues, without the slightest movement—no speaking, no swaying, no twitching fingers, not even any blinking eyelids, if possible. Have them hold this position for several seconds as they struggle to remain motionless.

Wherever it came from, this inspired idea serves three essential functions:

1) It enables the teacher/director to instantaneously regain the attention of an otherwise charged-up roomful of overly exuberant adolescents.

2) It creates the absolute silence needed to give the next set of instructions.

3) It offers young actors the opportunity to develop both an inward and an outward sense of self control. They learn to switch from madcap emoting to silent statues in the time it takes to say "Freeze!" They also begin to acquire mastery over their bodies, utilizing this difficult technique of remaining motionless for several moments at a time.

Exercise 38: STATUES

This activity is really a simpler version of the more challenging STATUES INTO SCENES (exercise 52), which moves into improvisational waters. In this less complicated exploration, have students pair up. Designate one person in each pair as the sculptor, the other as the clay. The clay's initial position is standing with head and arms down. The sculptor's objective is to mold and shape the clay into some interesting position appropriate to the clay's character in the play. Since this is another silent exercise (the clay is inanimate, of course, a lifeless block), the only way the sculptor can achieve her goal is by manipulating the clay. Let us imagine that the sculptor wants to fashion the clay into a crouching, fearful figure. She might begin by gently buckling the clay's knees and pushing down on the shoulders to obtain the desired crouch. Then she might ball the hands of the subject into fists, take the arms and move them from the subject's sides to a protective position crossing in front of the face. A slight tilt of the clay's head upward, and an altered facial expression with eyes wide and mouth slightly open could complete the statue.

The clay, of course, must be cooperative. It is all too easy to sabotage any sculptor's attempts by turning into "jello" or "concrete." If the sculptor raises the subject's arm into a pointing position, the clay must offer just enough resistance for the arm to stay there, not to flop back down. After the sculptor has completed the statue, it is always interesting to have the sculpture hold its position while all the artists take a brief tour of the room, admiring other sculptors' work. Then at a given signal, the statues should come to life, like Hermione in *The Winter's Tale*. This can be done either one at a time or simultaneously, with each statue now speaking some lines in character that are suggested by his or her sculpted pose.

This is a "touchy" exercise. Some students may feel uncomfortable being manipulated through touch into one position or another. Obviously, the sculptor must use good judgment—every class has one wise guy who may try to put his subject into some impossibly twisted, pretzel pose. He must also exercise as much sensitivity as possible. Handling the clay roughly or disrespectfully may result in exclusion from the activity.

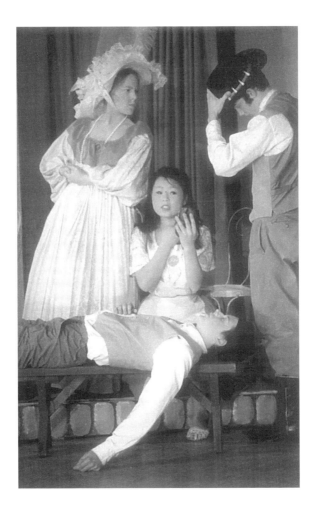

From The Madwoman of Chaillot – *10th grade production*

Chapter VII

Playing for Timing

No formula, no stage directions, no dogmatic as-sertions can ever teach young actors that all-too-elusive capacity known in the theater as timing. Only a few actors of any age have that unerring gift of knowing how long to hold a pause or how quickly to open a letter. Directors, however, must awaken within them some intuitive sense of timing; for whatever else a play is, it consists of a series of moments, some compressed and intense, like little ex-plosions, some lingering and sustained, like a violin's held final note.

Every one of these moments requires a director's decision. How quickly should Emily cross the stage to take her place with the other spirits in the third act of *Our Town*? How deliberately should Hamlet speak his "To be or not to be" soliloquy? How radically should the pace of *Cyrano de Bergerac's* poignant last scene at the nunnery shift from Cyrano's quiet revelation as Roxane's ever-faithful, anony-mous lover to his final, defiant outburst as he challenges Death to a duel? These, and a thousand other choices, alter the pulse of a play. If such moments are not consciously crafted and synchronized, they will create an impression, perhaps one akin to musicians in a symphony orchestra all playing their parts at different tempos. No matter how bril-liantly one virtuoso plays, the net effect will be cacophony.

Directors might think of themselves as conductors, approaching the movements of a play as musical passages. Their interpretation of the "dynamics"—the *legatos* and *andantes* and *ritardandos*—will transform a play from a static, undifferentiated piece to a vital and compelling experience.

I have found few actual exercises that cultivate this all-important sense of timing. Most of these moments need to be modulated in the give-and-take of rehearsal. One tries a scene at one pace, then sees that it drags on interminably or gallops away, trampling all possibility of subtlety or nuance in its path. And within the overall tempo of a scene, each character contributes a particular rhythm, every one of which requires careful orchestration, so that all these points and counterpoints can be appreciated in the course of a play.

One simple technique of finding the proper pace in any given scene is to deliberately speed up or slow down the action. The following exercise is good preparation.

Exercise 39: CHANGING SPEEDS

Have each of the participants think of any simple physical task or chore—watering a plant, sweeping the floor, setting the table, washing a window, folding clothes, clipping a hedge. They should perform their tasks first as deliberately as possibly, even in slow motion. Then they should repeat them at double speed, as if they were in a video going fast-forward. Finally, they should perform the actions a final time, somewhere between the extremes, now at a pace that seems to suit their particular characters' inner rhythms.

Exercise 40: FOUR-PHASE IMPROV

This is really a more advanced and challenging activity, partly because it calls upon an improvisational presence of mind; however, it may be one of the safest of improvisations, because the actors establish a "blueprint" for their interaction in preliminary stages. The exercise proceeds in four distinct phases:

1) Identify four or five volunteers and give them a setting/situation, for example:

> — musicians at a quartet rehearsal
> — construction workers on site
> — customers and employees at a diner
> — doctors/nurses in an operating room
> — baseball players positioned in the infield
> — mountain climbers near a summit

Give your volunteers about thirty seconds to come up with some rudimentary idea, some initial assignments of character to provide an initial direction for their scene. Now have the actors *mime* some interaction. Make sure all participants involve themselves. Allow two or three minutes for the scene to unfold, then call "Curtain!" when you see some reasonable ending point.

2) Ask the actors to repeat the scene as exactly as possible, incorporating as many gestures as they recall; however, this time their characters speak in *gibberish*. Gibberish seems to have a most liberating effect on young actors who otherwise become tongue-tied and paralyzed when asked to improvise. In this exercise, the gibberish augments the gestures already established in the mimed scene; students find they can use inflections and inventive vocal modulations to convey meaning without having to worry about the actual meaning.

3) Now students *translate their nonsense into English* and recreate the scene a third time. This may be one of the least "exposing" techniques for introducing improvisation, since the template for the scene has already been made through the two previous stages. Again, the objective here is to retain the gestures that animated the mimed version and the speaking patterns that energized the gibberish scene.

4) This last stage requires participants to perform the scene a final time, but at a radically different pace, either *in slow motion or at double speed*. If they choose the former, every aspect of the scene must slow down—their speaking rhythms will warp into the distorted delivery reminiscent of an old vinyl record played at 78 rpm instead of 45. Their gestures will look as if they are occurring underwater. Accelerating the scene will require that all actors synchronize their actions and speed up their reactions in the manner of the old Keystone Kops.

Exercise 41:   THE SPEED-THROUGH REHEARSAL
          The accelerated version of the FOUR-WAY IMPROV can also be used to great effect towards the end of any production. Usually a week or so before the actual performances, the play goes flat. The actors know their lines, where to move, and how. Yet the cast has lost touch with some of that original excitement of mounting a production and has not yet caught the slightly intoxicating, frenzied fever of the final days before opening night. In a word, rehearsals may have become mechanical.
          THE SPEED-THROUGH REHEARSAL can provide the perfect antidote to such lifelessness.   The objective is to perform the entire play in half the time it usually takes. This is, by any reasonable standards, a daft undertaking. Asking lethargic teenagers to suddenly act at twice the pace of normal life is certain to ignite resistance within the cast. That it does, but assuming the director can rouse the company to the challenge, THE SPEED-THROUGH also raises the whole energy level to new heights. It requires tremendous intensity on the part of the director; the tendency of the actors will be to slow down. They need to constantly be exhorted to keep the pace up. This usually means a good deal of screaming, "Faster! Keep it up! Get moving!" The rehearsal will be a madhouse; actors will be racing through their lines, bolting on and off the stage, crashing into one another, losing their composure as their

characters double over in laughter, losing any sense of subtlety in their characters or lines as they charge through the play. But the renewed vitality within the cast, their sheer delight in the resulting insanity, is worth any temporary loss of form or nuance.

The Power of the Pause

Young actors tend to butcher lines in two different ways: They either recite them in a labored, undifferentiated monotone, or they gallop through them facilely but without regard to meaning. Either extreme ignores the power of the pause to invest any given moment with significance. Teenagers generally do not care much for silence. Think only of the ubiquitous music playing in their rooms—they awaken to hip-hop; they fall asleep to oldies. My own teenage children have two automatic responses once they are in our car—fasten seat belt, turn on radio. It is not surprising that they might feel discomfort with even the smallest pause onstage. And yet, it is just there—between the spoken words, between the lines—that the real drama occurs. It enlarges our sense of Gloucester in *King Lear* when Lear says to the now blinded old man, "You see how the world goes," and Gloucester pauses before responding, "I see it . . . feelingly." (Act IV, scene vi) He has *felt* it first, and that feeling is communicated in the filled silence. The electrifying pause accompanying Helen Keller's growing realization that the water flowing out of the pump has a name fills us, too, with wonder and light.

How can students learn this truth of the theater? They need to see that virtually every exchange between characters needs to be mined for its dramatic potential. Furthermore, they need to learn that pauses have differing qualities. One character will pause after a question to formulate a cunningly deceptive answer, an Iago casting a net to tangle the mind of Othello—the pause filled with malicious intent. Another will pause after the truth breaks

84

in on him, as when Oedipus discovers his nightmarish fate—the pause of self-recognition. Still another character will hesitate when struck dumb by love, as Orlando does in *As You Like It* after Rosalind gives him her chain.

Sometimes an entire play can be summed up in a pause. I know of no more telling moment than when, at the end of *The Grapes of Wrath*—Frank Galati's marvelous adaptation of the Steinbeck novel—Rose of Sharon and her mother stumble into a barn sheltering a starving man and his small son. Rose of Sharon is still weak from having given birth to a stillborn child and from having to vacate, because of the rising floodwaters, the boxcar they called home. The man lies on the floor of the barn, semiconscious. His child pleads with the two women to find something for his father to eat or drink so he will not die. At this moment, Ma turns to Rose of Sharon and wordlessly asks the question—"Will you help him?" In the ensuing pause, we experience all of Rose of Sharon's past pain—the abandonment of her husband, the humiliation of being jobless and homeless, the loss of her child only moments before. We also feel another impulse rising in her—the desire to give to another human being who is worse off than she is the only thing she has left to give. In this pause the entire ill-fated journey of the Joad family is ennobled; Rose of Sharon simply says, "Yes," then goes to the man, bends over him, and guides his mouth to her bared, milk-laden breast.

The success or failure of such a profound moment will ultimately depend upon whether or not young actors can summon the inner forces to fill these pauses with the appropriate substance. The next section offers a number of exercises to help student infuse such moments, and even the entire atmosphere of a scene, with depth and resonance.

From Museum – *12th Grade production*

Chapter VIII

Charging the Atmosphere

How can one describe the experience of walking into a high school gymnasium late in the fourth quarter of a tournament basketball game? Thunderous waves of "De—fense! De—fense!" compete with a chorus of "We will, we will ROCK YOU!" from the other side of the floor. The whole building seems to vibrate as the fans scream, curse, stomp, and cheer with every swish of the ball through the net, every blown whistle, every stolen pass. The atmosphere is electrifying!

Now consider a scene in another large building, where vaulted, domed ceilings soar six stories over the heads of these spectators. Light filters in, illuminating the huge, stained glass figures as well as the curls of incense smoke wafting heavenward. Candles flicker around the altar. Except for a cough or the rustle of someone shifting positions in the pews, people sit in silence; only a priest's voice chanting prayers in Latin breaks the heavy hush that bows people's heads and curtails conversation.

The somber atmosphere during a service in a cathedral stands in stark contrast to a championship game in a gymnasium—that much seems clear. But what really creates the difference? Does the space always dictate the mood of the people inhabiting it? Could the atmosphere of that same gymnasium be permeated with the solemnity of the cathedral if some religious ceremony were held there?

For actors, addressing these questions cannot be a matter of mere speculation. They cannot readily move their playing space into a burning building if they want to convey panic, or onto the boardwalk in Atlantic City if they want to simulate the exhilaration of adults suddenly liberated. No, actors must transform a neutral space into every imaginable setting. And, unless they have at their disposal elaborate sets, sophisticated sound and lighting effects, and splendid costumes, most of this theatrical magic must be generated through the imaginations of the actors themselves.

The success of exercises focusing on atmospheres depends upon:

1) Attentive silence, at least initially. A more advanced variation involving dialogue comes later.

2) Collaboration. While one actor onstage alone can certainly create a palpable mood, that same atmosphere will not become as tangible if it is not a shared experience of all actors onstage.

3) Gradual intensification. What begins as a dim awareness—the seed of a doubt, perhaps—blossoms into raging suspicion.

4) Internalization. What begins as an objective feeling or mood in their surroundings by degrees affects and, eventually, transforms the actors. What was without moves within—as opposed to the actors' externalizing some gnawing feeling.

Exercise 42: WEATHER EXTREMES
As with our other dramatic sequences, it seems most effective to begin with more "concrete" and accessible

physical atmospheres. Extreme weather conditions provide good material. Ask students to close their eyes and imagine themselves in a blizzard. Then have them open their eyes and move, hunched and huddled against the biting gale and the stinging snow. As they struggle to keep their footing in the deepening drifts, they believe they see a dwelling in the distance. They stagger towards the cabin and finally reach the cabin door. With a final surge of strength they pry the door open and fall into the warmth of the shelter. Allow them to experience the contrast of this interior space. The muffled howls of the wind outside only accentuate the relief they feel to be out of the storm. They may take off their wet coats and move to the fireplace, where the radiating warmth and the golden glow of the flames gradually fill the room and the weary travelers with a sense of well-being.

You must, of course, guide young actors through such experiences with a vivid narration. The more detailed the guidance can be, the more likely the students will enter fully into the imaginative space.

Another polarity would be to lead them from a swamp walk through the thickest, most humid jungle to a parching, desert trek. Other, albeit less climatic contrasts, might include having students move

— from a dark to a light place, such as an inky, dank cavern through a tunnel to a blindingly bright mountain summit
— from a confined to an expansive area, such as a crowded elevator to an alpine meadow
— from a hot to a cold place, such as the rim of an active volcano to an ice floe
— from isolated to peopled, such as a secluded tropical beach to Fifth Avenue in New York City at the end of the work day

> — from a frenetic to a tranquil setting, such as a
> New Year's Eve disco party to
> an ashram

Although products of imagination, all these situations share in common physical environments that students can materialize through their creative efforts. Conjuring emotional atmospheres is a far subtler, but ultimately far more fruitful, challenge.

Exercise 43: EMOTIONAL ATMOSPHERES

Students might begin by walking normally around the room; allow them to gradually become aware that a whiff of uncertainty hangs in the air. Now they move differently to reflect this growing apprehension they feel all around them—their gestures become more guarded, their steady gaze becomes a series of watchful, even furtive, glances. Perhaps this atmosphere congeals into suspicion, a feeling that becomes so oppressive that they begin to glare accusingly at fellow classmates—no one can be trusted. They may edge towards the shadowy corners of the room, the better to avoid being followed, the better to observe suspects. Participants now express through every darting shift of the eyes, every jumpy gesture, every anxious breath, the rampant suspicion in the atmosphere. Perhaps this is the air that millions of Americans breathed during the McCarthy era in the early 1950s, when "there was a Commie under every bed."

Many other emotional atmospheres or attitudes can be explored:

> — irritation to anger to rage
> — distress to depression to anguish
> — anxiety to fear to terror
> — interest to acute attention to awe
> — uncertainty to confusion to chaos

— resolve to courage to foolhardiness
— cleverness to deception
— indifference to neglect to abandonment
— anticipation to enthusiasm to exhilaration
— wishfulness to envy to covetousness
— courtesy to kindness to benevolence
— interest to attraction to passion
— teasing to ridicule
— pride to arrogance
— frustration to exasperation

Exercise 44: SWITCHING ATMOSPHERES

This activity requires a good deal of inner flexibility. Instead of a one-way intensification of a particular mood, have students begin working with one atmosphere, then gradually transform it to its opposite. For example, you might establish with them an air of resignation in the room, and then slowly shift the mood to determination. Or you might switch from an atmosphere of congeniality to one of hostility. A few other possible polarities include the following:

— from dejection to hope
— from relaxation to tension
— from cynicism to awe
— from isolation to unity
— from indifference to compassion
— from boredom to fascination
— from timidity to confidence
— from selfishness to saintliness

Exercise 45 : PERSONAL ATMOSPHERES

Usually actors working collaboratively can color a scene with an overriding atmosphere. But that general, pervasive mood will often become an amalgam of more localized and conflicting personal atmospheres. For example, in *The Skin of Our Teeth*; the overall atmosphere in

Act II is one of rising panic as the deluge approaches. Yet Sabina, Miss Atlantic City and archetypal goldigger, has but one objective—to lure George Antrobus away from his wife and family by any means necessary. The aura of a seductress radiates from Sabina. George, on the other hand, begins the scene irritated at his wife, a feeling that grows into open hostility at her attempts to keep him on a short leash when he wants to have some fun. When his vexation encounters Sabina's temptation, George does not stand a chance. Perhaps as much as any other factor, it is this clash of personal atmospheres that helps to create riveting tension onstage.

Young actors can explore personal atmospheres in the most elementary way, by performing actions similar to those in CHANGING SPEEDS—putting on a sweater, eating a sandwich, blowing up a balloon, hanging a picture, feeding the cat, changing a lightbulb, dusting a shelf, hammering a stake, scrambling eggs. Now, however, the actors complete their task under the influence of a particular, subjective mood. Have them feed the cat first ashamedly, then purposefully, coldly, violently, enthusiastically. Each new variation demands that the actors extend their mood beyond themselves, so that they color the very air around them, like an aura.

Other possible portrayals include performing some action in the following ways:

awkwardly	gently	haughtily
despondently	foolishly	vengefully
sentimentally	tediously	pensively
tauntingly	frantically	fearfully
distractedly	eagerly	skeptically
spitefully	meditatively	carelessly
longingly	grandly	intimately

This activity can be a springboard to some advanced improvisations, as most clearly seen in the following exercise.

Exercise 46: EMOTIONAL MIRRORS

The idea here is to enact a scene wherein two or more participants mirror each other's changing emotional states. Have one actor—let us call her Rose—begin a scene with a specific mood in mind, such as despair. She begins talking with her best friend about how circumstances are compelling her to leave her home and a newly discovered, still tender relationship. At first, her best friend—Cecilia— mirrors Rose's despair. Then Cecilia suddenly brightens as she receives an inspiration—why can't they travel together, get away from the overcrowded city, and pay a visit to Rose's father, who has a cabin in the north woods? Rose instantly brightens as well, reflecting Cecilia's irrepressible cheerfulness, and even suggests bringing along their best male friend, Tony, mostly for his capacity to make them both laugh.

The scenario may sound very familiar to Shakespeare buffs; it is a thinly disguised update of the moment in *As You Like It* when Rosalind is accused of treason by her uncle, Duke Fredrick, and banished from the kingdom. Celia, daughter of the Duke and Rosalind's best friend, attempts to lift Rosalind's melancholy mood by suggesting they disguise themselves and go to the forest of Arden to reunite with Rosalind's exiled father. At once, Rosalind's spirits rise as she savors the possibilities both of dressing up as a man to protect them, and of luring Touchstone, the court clown, to accompany them. The scene ends with both young ladies bubbling with elation and anticipation over their secret plans.

Emotional mirroring requires participants to be keenly attuned to one another. Whatever mood is initially established by one actor, the other actor immediately reinforces. When one of them begins to transform the atmosphere to its opposite—say, from despair to elation, or from cynicism to wonder—the other player follows suit. This exercise, along with MOOD SWING described below, are most challenging activities; usually, only older high school students possess the inner resources to satisfy the demands of the activity.

Exercise 47: MOOD SWING

Ask one participant to think of a particular mood to work with—say, boredom. Another actor may be given a mood of excitement to convey. In the course of a short dialogue, the objective of the exercise is to gradually exchange one's given atmosphere for the other actor's. Here is an example:

A: I can't stand another minute behind the counter of this boring nursery. We haven't had a customer in four hours.

B: Hey, look at this! The seeds I planted last week are sprouting! My babies are growing!

A: It doesn't interest me in the least. My feet are killing me.
B: Look at that! The stem is sending out bifurcated leaves already.

A: Bi-fur what?

B: Bifurcated. Little leaves split in two. You remember from botany class. See?

A: You don't have to shove the pot into my . . . hey . . . you just planted these a few days ago? What kind of plants are these?

B: Zucchini, I think. Or are they sunflowers? I should have labeled them.

A: They're very cute. The leaves look like little forked tongues. I love the way they . . . oops! Oh, no. I thought you were holding it from the bottom.

B: I wasn't. You grabbed it away from me. Now they're ruined.

A: No, they're not. Look, we can sweep up the soil and put them in another pot and . . .

B: Forget it. They'll die now.

A: Wait! Look! I'm replanting them. They'll be as good as before! See? They're standing tall and singing, "It's good to be green and alive!" Look!

B: It's no use. I'm not interested.

This is a more advanced exercise not only because it involves verbal improvisation, but also because it requires tremendous sensitivity on the part of both actors. They both need to establish their own, diametrically opposite moods, ideally by showing, not telling, the audience what they are. Then they must exchange atmospheres so artfully that, in retrospect, the audience might not be able to identify when the switch began.

When working with a production, the director may help young actors ascertain which personal atmospheres may help them develop certain soul qualities. Take, for example, the scene in *Twelfth Night* when Malvolio appears before Olivia, cross-gartered, yellow-stockinged, and smiling like a lunatic, as he mistakenly believes she instructed him to do in the forged letter he finds. An air of great expectation sets up the scene, as the forgers savor the extremes to which Malvolio might go in his ardor for his unsuspecting employer. Malvolio exudes the confidence of a chosen one; his personal atmosphere conveys all the suppressed lust he has stored up for Olivia. "Sweet lady, ho ho!" By contrast, Olivia's mood shifts from initial shock over his bizarre appearance to growing concern that he may be ill. "Wilt thou go to bed, Malvolio?" And, his judgment utterly clogged by his own vanity and desire, he completely misunderstands the import of Olivia's words. "To bed? Ay, sweetheart and I'll come to thee." (Act III, scene iv) Such conflicting personal atmospheres can create the same kind of dynamic interchange as two storm fronts colliding.

Working with atmospheres can be of immense assistance to young actors in helping them to fabricate not only a setting, but also a palpable mood. Just as dry ice vapor or cigarette smoke densifies the quality of the atmosphere onstage, so students can learn to charge the air of any given scene in a perceptible way. If they can materialize and sustain such moods, they may also one day encounter during a play that quasi-transcendent feeling actors live for. Like an exhausted swimmer who feels buoyed up by the surrounding waters, actors onstage can also experience an almost indescribable feeling of being borne aloft, elevated by the very milieu through which they move. Such is the magic that atmospheres can create.

Chapter IX

Finding Each Other–Ensemble Playing

By their very nature, adolescents are seekers. In a culture that often appears devoid of purpose or coherence or community, they are desperately searching for meaning and relationship. Perhaps part of drama's appeal for young people is that it offers—indeed, requires—actors to incorporate both meaning and relationship into their efforts. As hackneyed as it has become, the axiom that drama is the most social of arts is founded upon a fundamental truth of the theater. Every production we mount relies upon the creation of a "concentrated community." For the three or four weeks that we work on the play, the players must act in concert; i.e, they must not only acknowledge each other, they must both *nourish*, as well as *be nourished* by, each other. If they do not genuinely respond to one another's characters onstage, scenes will ring hollow, moments will lack authenticity.

From the very beginning, we try to obliterate the notion that this or that role is some star vehicle. No portrayal is going to touch an audience if an actor operates in a vacuum onstage. Every character must be seen as a crucial part of an organic totality. A number of activities can be employed to underscore this approach.

Exercise 48: SITTING WITHOUT A CHAIR

Although students will see this exercise as pure fun, even the slightest bit of reflection will help them recognize its emblematic value. Arrange the cast in a tight circle, all standing and facing clockwise. Have them take small side-ways steps towards the center of the circle until they are as snugly situated next to one another as possible, one person's back touching another's front. At the director's signal, all participants slowly and simultaneously sit down on the knees of the person directly behind them. Done success-fully, the circle will form one enormous group chair, en-tirely self-supporting.

This is an easy exercise to undermine for the sake of a "group spill." One prankster who decides to miss his or her perch will cause everyone to take a tumble. How-ever, even such foolishness can be instructive in this case. It only takes one actor who misses an entrance or drops out of character or forgets a critical prop to sabotage an entire scene. No exercise is better suited for demonstrat-ing the absolute interdependence of every cast member.

Exercise 49: MAKING A MACHINE

Have one person begin by standing in the center of a circle and performing some simple, repeatable motion. The initiator establishes a regular rhythm with this move-ment and continues unwaveringly throughout the exercise, or until instructed differently by you. Then have another student join in by adding a motion that is somehow related to the first person's, but without any physical contact. The rhythm of the second participant's movement need not be the same as the initiator's, but it must bear some relation-ship to the initial beat. Direct subsequent students to con-tinue to add moveable parts to this "machine," always in-tegrating their movements in some inventive fashion.

Until the last actor completes the apparatus, have the machine parts move silently. When all students have joined, ask them to begin making the sounds they imagine their parts would make. The ensuing cacophony is always entertaining. As a final challenge, you might alter the speed of the mechanism by asking the initiator to speed up or slow down until the device comes to grinding halt. All parts of the machine then must adjust accordingly to keep their movements and sounds synchronized.

Demonstration – Exercise #49

A variation of this free-form machine is to have students become the necessary parts of a familiar machine or other object with moveable parts; some memorable creations have included an automobile (complete with somersaulting "tires"), a washing machine, a sailboat, an old-fashioned record player, a typewriter (remember those?), an oil derrick, and a backhoe. Some students may have to assume the roles of human beings to operate the device.

Exercise 50: GO ORGANIC!

An "organic" alternative to the machine idea involves asking students as a group to create some living (or at least moving) form in nature—a tree, an elephant, a volcano. For the elephant, a number of students might become, for example, the body, four others the legs, another one the tail, still another the trunk. Flora can be most effectively depicted if represented as growing over time, from seed to sprout to sapling to, say, full-grown oak.

Exercise 51: CHARACTER BIOGRAPHIES

Earlier exercises (such as Exercise 34: GETTING TO KNOW ME) asked students to enlarge the characters they play by activating their imaginations. However, actors worked primarily as individuals then, not interactively. This activity calls upon participants to assist one another in improvised scenes exploring their characters. First, have all actors imagine their characters as six-year-olds.

After they picture their characters as children, instruct participants to begin playing together as six-year-olds during a school recess or at a park on a Saturday afternoon. Whatever activity they choose—jumping rope, playing tag, building with blocks, playing house, slaying dragons—they should always attempt to portray their characters' fledging individualities.

While you can guide them into other significant, improvisational moments of their characters' lives—for example, first love, some tragic loss, wedding day—an essential phase is to have them imagine themselves towards the end of their lives, when their characters are, say, eighty-six-years-old. Have your actors pair up, sit down somewhere, and in character, reminisce about their lives. In their improvised conversation, they might disclose their happiest and saddest moments, their greatest triumph, their deepest unfulfilled dream. Perhaps they will even share a secret they have been carrying for decades, because they wish to unburden themselves before they die.

Exercise 52: STATUES INTO SCENES

As they did in the simpler version (Exercise 38: STATUES), students assume the roles of sculptors and clay.

In this exercise, one sculptor has two clay pieces to work with. The artist's aim is to think of the characters portrayed by these two people in the play. Then, using the same molding technique as described in STATUES, the sculptor fashions his two figures so that their positions place them in some physical relationship to one another. One character may be in the frozen pose of trying to kiss the other, while the other character may be positioned to ward off such unwanted advances.

After the sculpture is completed, ask the statues to hold their poses while artists admire each other's work. Then, at a given signal, have the statues come to life. Taking their cues from their relative positions, the figures should improvise a brief scene in character, either one pair at a time or simultaneously. It doesn't really matter if these two characters don't play a scene together in the actual play. Any interaction stimulated by this exercise will add depth and amplitude to the characters.

Exercise 53: WALKING AS OTHER CHARACTERS

This is another activity that requires the entire cast to act cooperatively and also serves to broaden each actor's understanding of the entire cast of characters. Ask one student to sit down and be an attentive observer as everyone else begins to walk around the room (and perhaps even speaks) as the observer's character. Often the student sitting out will notice one or another classmate's inventive movement or gesture that can be incorporated into the actual character. Over a couple of rehearsals, each actor can benefit from the experience of watching the entire cast assume his or her role.

Exercise 54: SOUND/WORD SYMPHONY

Ask the entire cast to form two or three horizontal lines facing you, while you act as symphony conductor. One line of students might sit on the floor, another in chairs behind the first, and a third line might stand behind the chairs. Ask the sitting participants to think of a sound that expresses the quintessential quality of their characters. Those standing might think of a word that sums up their characters' philosophy of life. When everyone has in mind a particular sound or word, listen to each student's contribution in succession.

Once you know what sort of raw material you have to work with, the symphony can begin. Point to one student whose sound might be "Grrr," and give him a tempo so he can utter his "Grrr" in some continual rhythm. Then bring in other sounds or words simply by pointing to students and giving them counterpoints or syncopated beats to follow. When all the parts have been introduced, you can play with the "music" by asking for fortissimo from some sections, piano from others. With a point and a wave of your hand, the word section might be silent altogether, while the sound section swells to a crashing crescendo. Or perhaps three or four soloists could be selected to highlight a particular theme. The direction the symphony takes is limited only by your imagination.

Exercise 55: ALTERNATING WORDS

Break your cast into pairs and have them, in character, compose a letter to another character in the play. However, they may only "write" the letter by speaking aloud, and by alternating words, without prior planning. The first character may say "Dear," the second, "Bottom." First: I— Second: must— First: inform— Second: you— First: that—(in continued alternation) my—mistress—considers—you—a—godlike—jackass—with—your—long—hairy—ears—and—noble—but—drippy—nostrils.

This kind of improvisation demands that each actor be attuned to the other, so that the letter can have some coherence. However, an even more complex variation of this exercise can take unexpected twists.

Exercise 56: FOUR-HEADED CHARACTER
            CONFESSIONALS

Choose four actors, who will become "four mouths" of a single character in the play. The character may be one currently portrayed by one of the selected students, but that is not essential. You should instruct this four-headed character to improvise some answer to any of the following, revealing questions:

— What is your most embarrassing memory?
— After whom do you secretly lust?
— What would you do differently in your life if
        you could?
— In what ways have you changed since you were
        a child?
— In what ways do you most resemble your
        mother/father?
— What is the nicest deed you ever did?
— Is there anything you would die for?
— What do you do when no one else is around?

Once the question is posed, the four-headed character can answer by again speaking only single words in succession. For example, a four-headed response from Malvolio to the question "What do you like most about yourself?" might go as follows (each mouth says only one word, ideally linking it to the previous words, then passes the sentence along):

My—toes—are—among—my—favorite—treasures.—I—love—to—dip—them—in—wet—cement—and—delicately—tapdance—on—my—mistress'—forehead.—Another—of—my—best—features—is—my—right—eyebrow.—Can—you—appreciate—how—it—arches—like—a—great—banana?

The four-person commentary usually makes even less sense than this silly example. However, the substance of the scene is less important than the ensemble feeling engendered by the demands of the exercise. At its best, this activity can have participants and audience alike on the edge of their seats. Every word spoken can become a trigger that shoots the entire thought sequence into some totally unexpected direction.

Exercise 57: DUBBING

Sometimes young actors find it difficult to integrate speech and gesture into their characters. Either they stand woodenly, declaiming their lines, or their hands gyrate and flap in unconscious accompaniment. Dubbing awakens actors to the need for purposeful gestures that enhance, rather than distract from, the spoken word. At the same time, the activity of dubbing fosters an unusual form of collaboration between cast members.

A preliminary exercise might be called VERBAL MIRRORING. Have students stand in pairs facing each other. One initiates some conversation, but speaks very slowly, while the other person simultaneously attempts to say exactly the same words with the same inflections. Skilled partners become so adept at this simultaneous speaking that an observer cannot easily distinguish which one is leading the conversation.

The primary dubbing exercise calls for an actor and a dubber, who will speak or animatedly read the actor's lines from somewhere behind the actor. As the dubber reads, the actor may mouth the lines, but his or her main focus will be to gesture expressively, in consonance with the lines being spoken. If the dubber weeps, the actor's gestures must convey the act of crying. If the dubber screams, the actor needs to intensify his or her movements to communicate the passion behind the words. Hearing someone else speak a character's lines nearly always awakens an actor to new dimensions and possibilities.

Exercise 58: ENACTING A STORY

One of our favorite theatrical activities represents the height of ensemble work. Choose a story that is short—no more than two or three pages—colorful, and full of imagery. Russian folktales have proven ideal for our purposes, such as "Two from the Sack," or "Treasure," or "The Crafty Peasant." A group could also enact a dream that an actor retells, or for that matter, some biographical incident. With these latter suggestions, you should be aware that the direction of the class is straying towards psychodrama, which can be fraught with both exciting possibilities and potentially explosive personal reactions.

Whatever the source of the story, this exercise is best done in three distinct stages:

1) Read or tell the story to the group after alerting them that they will be retelling it after you are finished. The more animated and vivid your presentation, the more likely the students are able to recall it accurately.

2) Have the listeners now sit in a circle, with each student recreating a segment of the tale. If someone forgets a detail or scrambles the chronology, others are allowed to gently correct the narrator—not "No, you idiot. First he took a bath and then the greedy mother replaced the magic sack with a common one. How could you be such an airhead?" Try to divide the segments more or less equally among your participants so every student has an opportunity to relate part of the tale. Again, their retelling is based on how well they listened—the story is not being passed around the circle to be read.

3) The third stage is potentially one of the most stimulating and creative ensemble acting challenges we know. Explain to the group that their final task is to now dramatize the tale spontaneously, that is, without any time to rehearse, assign parts, and so on. Not only that—in this enactment, actors will portray not only human characters, but every other significant element in the story, animate

or inanimate—a hut, a carriage, the waves of the sea, a pig, a hat, a table, the north wind, gold pieces—whatever needs depicting to relate the story as colorfully as possible. Furthermore, since they will have no way of planning the play in any rational, orderly way, any one or two or even three people may jump up at any moment to become the narrator or the main character or the oven or the goat. That is fine—multiple portrayals only add to the wackiness of this chaotic, preposterous, and often ingenious piece of theater. The only requirement is that the whole group be involved in the dramatization and that they stick to the original storyline more or less faithfully. We hope that each participant will be sensitive enough not to dominate the play. One person may begin as a narrator, then suddenly become a broomstick, transform instantly into one of three old crones, and end up being a tombstone.

This same technique might be used to enliven an actual play rehearsal, when the cast hits that predictable low point late in the production process. Allow the actors to portray any character except their own, and all of the other essential props as well. Again, it makes no difference if two or three people go onstage to play one role. It will breathe new life into even the most moribund of productions.

Exercise 59: GIVE AND TAKE

Young actors can attempt this difficult exercise, but older adolescents—ages 17 and up—usually have more success. Divide your stage into two acting areas, and have two or three actors sit around a table in each area. Give each group some topic to discuss that might stimulate a lively conversation, even an argument: the relative merits of tennis vs. golf, of dogs vs. cats, of classical music vs. heavy metal, of living in the country vs. living in the city. Each group should have a different topic. Then have both groups begin their conversation simultaneously. The effect, of course, will be "cacophony," until you instruct one group to "Turn down the volume," while the other group carries the primary action onstage. Then, at a given signal, give the softer-speaking group permission to take the focus. Their conversation gets louder and more animated while the other group's dialogue fades into the background but still continues softly. This switching can continue back and forth, as the actors become evermore adroit at taking and giving up the limelight.

The exercise helps young people appreciate the sometimes subtle but constant shifting of focus that takes place on stage. In this regard theatrical movement is not unlike the action of a baseball game. The primary focus, of course, is on the ball, and whatever player is closest to it. But every other player is continually making almost imperceptible adjustments in position, always focused on the flight of the ball, always moving in anticipation of its next bounce. At the crack of the bat, a player more removed from the immediate action—say, the right fielder—suddenly takes the stage as the ball heads into his territory. He fields the ball, throws the runner out trying to stretch a single into a double, doffs his cap to acknowledge the spectators' appreciative applause, and returns to his unsung status in the shadow of the bleachers.

Onstage, as well, inexperienced actors need to learn when to take the limelight and when to relinquish it for the greater good of a scene. The most aware supporting actors will strike that balance between overacting and unresponsiveness. The actor in the background whose antics distract from the central action sabotages a scene just as surely as the catatonic character who does not react at all to his or her fellow players. The one diffuses the audience's focus; the other creates a vacuum by sucking energy away from the dynamic of the play.

From Museum *– 12th grade production*

Chapter X

On a Highwire Without a Net:
Other Improvisational Ideas

So many of the exercises we have gathered from various sources, or have invented, were designed to achieve three aims:

1) to liberate students from the natural anxieties of appearing foolish,
2) to give them confidence that their imaginations are rich and boundless resources for their acting, and
3) to experience the magic of working collaboratively with others to create theatrical truths out of illusion.

To accomplish the first objective, I have already strongly recommended that all your students do many of these exercises simultaneously. When everyone involved is acting foolish, no one feels foolish. However, at some point students should also experience the exhilaration that can arise when working on the "highwire without a net," that is, improvising for an audience. Some students (and frankly, some directors, too) break out in a cold sweat whenever they think of having to improvise in front of others. It is certainly a more frightening prospect than prepared public speaking, which, we have always been told, creates more anxiety in most people than swimming with sharks. Yet if the audience consists of fellow classmates, and if the exercises can be artfully arranged in a sequence that gradually "en-courages" young actors to take chances, the anxiety usually associated with improvisation can be transformed into sheer excitement. The sense of risk one feels in improvisational work can kindle in young people an almost supernatural awareness of the present moment and of the people onstage with whom they create each moment.

I have never walked a tightrope without a net, but I rock climbed over a period of twenty years. The parallels between rock climbing and improvising are striking. Both involve an acute sense of exposure—one, of course, more physical. At the same time, the perception of peril in both cases intensifies the climber's/actor's senses, and most especially the sense of concentration. One's heightened awareness of the surface of the rock face becomes microscopic; even the tiniest nub of an outcropping, the smallest crack, can become the next toehold or fingerhold. That same alertness applies to improvisation as well. Participants must be constantly attentive to any opportunity that might link the present instant to the preceding and succeeding moments in some organic way. Improvising actors also quickly learn that they are inextricably connected to their fellow performers. Every word one speaks, every gesture one makes, affects the others; indeed, it can alter the very direction of a scene, so it becomes imperative for them to be attuned to each other. Climbers, also, are quite literally joined to one another. The rope is their lifeline, sometimes even their means of communication. For safety's sake, they must develop an acute sensitivity to the movements of the people belaying above or below them.

Of course, for climbers the rope does act as that safety net. If they have taken proper precautions—checked their equipment, climbed "within themselves" and not recklessly, trusted their intuitions and their fellow climbers—they will return to earth not only unscathed, but maybe even enlarged for having overcome more than mere gravity. Is there an equivalent lifeline for actors who enter into the risky realm of improvisation? There is, but it is intangible.

Every climber has had the experience of being frozen on the rock face—no move appears possible beyond a sliver of a ledge up to the left. Legs begin to shake, forearms cramp, as the climber begins to question, "What am I doing up here, anyway? This is crazy. I'm going to fall." However, the veteran climber will swing up to the ledge without much hesitation, knowing that a new possibility will present itself that was not discernible below. That is precisely the situation actors can find themselves in at some critical moment of an improvisation. They reach a dead end in some scene, and the temptation becomes overpowering to freeze or to drop out of character and say, "I can't do this." However, if they can only develop the confidence to make that blind move, new possibilities open up that they never saw before taking the risk.

Exercise 60: BLIND OFFERS

In Keith Johnstone's invaluable book *Impro*, he describes this activity as a critical, preliminary exercise for any actors interested in becoming adept at improvisation. One of the fundamental principles of improvisational work is that when one actor makes an "offer," that is, suggests a direction in a scene, the other actors onstage must not block or reject the offer. For example, if one person says, "Where's your wife?" the other doesn't respond with, "I don't have a wife." Otherwise, the scene stops dead at that point, because the second actor has invalidated the first actor's offer. However, if the second person builds upon the initial idea and replies with a conspiratorial whisper, "She's hiding in the closet," we now have the basis for a most promising scene.

The following, simple exercise helps students to accept such creative leads from their fellow actors. Ask participants to pair up, and have one person strike some interesting pose—maybe she assumes a batting stance and then freezes. Her partner makes some adjustment to her original position—perhaps he moves the bat so that the batter hits herself on the head, or he places both of her hands in a "hands up, this is a stick-up" pose. Whatever the second person does, the first accepts the alteration and says, without fail, "Thank you." Then the partners switch roles; now the second actor begins by assuming another intriguing position, and the first actor somehow modifies it, followed by another "Thank you." In this way, each participant is accepting the other's offer. It is a short step from this exercise to an extended improvisation in which all the actors must build upon each other's initiatives.

Exercise 61: SLAP SNAP

As an elementary warm-up for more advanced improvisational work, have students stand in a circle and begin a rhythm in unison. The most common rhythm is to slap both hands simultaneously on one's thighs (first beat), then clap hands (second beat), then snap right hand fingers (third beat), and finally snap left hand fingers (fourth beat). Once a regular rhythm has been established, the leader says any word on the fourth beat—for example, "submarine." The next person in the circle must take the last letter of that word—in this case, "e"—and start his word with it—say, "elbow," WITHOUT BREAKING THE RHYTHM. The next person must begin with the "w", and so the game continues, with the last letter of the previous word determining the beginning of the next.

If spontaneity is both the lifeblood and blood-chilling ingredient of improvisational work, this game offers a gentle introduction to the experience of reacting without premeditation. With so little time to deliberate or plot out a strategy, SLAP SNAP forces participants to stay absolutely focused in the present moment. It is virtually impossible to have the security of plotting out some word strategy in advance.

Exercise 62: ALPHABET SCENES

A more advanced and challenging development of the SLAP SNAP game involves two intrepid volunteers, who either choose or are given some situation by the group; Viola Spolin would call it a "Who" and a "Where." In this case, let us say that the suggested location is a jungle and that the actors are explorers. Then the group throws out a letter of the alphabet, say, "P." The only rule the actors must follow is that, beginning with P, each line they speak in alternation must begin with the next letter of the alphabet. As an illustration:

He: **P**lease hand me that machete. It's getting pretty thick and scary in front of us.

She: **Q**uiet! I think I hear something moving off to our right.

He: **R**un for it!

She: **S**o now you want to run? What kind of explorer are you, anyway?

He: **T**errified! I'm the terrified kind. I'm not really an explorer.

She: **U**h. . .what did you say?

He: **V**eterinarian. Graduated three years ago from PU. I'm a wing specialist.

She: **W**hy didn't you tell me this before?

He: **X**cellent question (this is an allowable bend
ing of the rules). Because I like to travel, and
I love your perfume.

She: (flattered) **Y**ou do? It's called. . ."Jungle Fever". . .

He: **Z**ebras have the same arousing scent!

And so on. The scene ends when the actors have completed the alphabet cycle and returned to their original starting letter.

Exercise 63: LET'S DO THIS!
Another very safe group improvisation requires
one person to suggest performing some simple action, such
as, "Let's ride a bicycle," whereupon everyone in the group
enthusiastically chimes in, "Yes, let's," and immediately
begins to mime bike riding. At any moment after that action has been established, another person can randomly
call out, "Let's. . .dive for abalone," which prompts the rest
of the group to respond heartily, "Yes, let's!" Then, everyone moves directly from bike riding to miming an underwater search. The only caution here is that, teenagers being teenagers, someone might suggest the most inappropriate action, such as "Let's take each other's clothes off!"
At that point you might want to intercede with a forceful
"LET'S NOT!" and suggest another, less risque action.

Exercise 64: WHAT ARE YOU DOING?
Have the actors pair up, and ask one to begin miming some recognizable action—brushing one's teeth, jumping rope, flipping pancakes. Have the other person observe
for a moment, then ask, "What are you doing?" The first
actor continues to brush her teeth but then says she is doing something totally unrelated— "I'm stamping out a

forest fire." That is the cue for her partner to immediately begin performing the action just described. As soon as her partner starts stamping out an imaginary fire, the actor who had been brushing her teeth stops that activity and asks the fire-stamper, "What are you doing?" Again the person stamping out the forest fire suggests an entirely different action, such as, "I'm sneezing uncontrollably," whereupon the person who had asked the question must begin miming one sneeze after another. In this manner, the pair performs a quick succession of actions based on each partner's imagination.

It doesn't take very long for young people to discover the power that they exert over their partners in this exercise. One may say, while miming the activity of bowling, "I'm standing on my head," thus compelling his partner to attempt that feat. Teachers should be alert to the escalation of potentially embarrassing or physically impossible mime suggestions.

Exercise 65: IT'S TUESDAY!

Whenever you find yourself confronted with students who hold back when they need to emote, who play too "small" when they need to "get some size," this exercise, also borrowed from *Impro*, is the perfect icebreaker. Again, have your actors pair up. Ask the first to make some exceedingly bland and neutral observation, such as "It's Tuesday" or "The clock stopped" or "Your shoe is untied." The more innocuous the statement, the better. Now ask the second actor to begin overreacting to the initial comment in somewhat the following manner:

> (Suddenly panic-stricken, looks down at his sneakers in horror.) "Oh, no! Not again! It can't be untied again!! (Trembling uncontrollably)
> That's the sixth time in the last ten minutes! Who is doing this to me? (Now dropping to his knees,

screaming) What malicious, unseen hand is tortur-
ing me this way? (Hysterically beating his breast) I
can't go on like this, I . . ."

At this point, the hysterical person suddenly re-
gains control and calmly makes another dispassion
ate observation: " . . . see that you are standing next
to the fishbowl." Then it is the first actor's turn to
react in the most melodramatic and overly exaggerated manner possible:

(Immediately in the throes of despair) "Of course,
I am, you insensitive block. (Beginning to weep).
And why am I standing here? Do you see any fish
in there? No, of course you don't. (Now sobbing)
That's because she's gone . . . gone . . . gone. Gone
forever. (Doubling over inconsolably) And she'll
never, ever, ever, ever, ever, ever come back. There's
a . . . (now calmly) peanut on the floor."

Rarely have I used an exercise that achieved its aim
in such an entertaining fashion. Once students see that over-
the-edge exaggeration is exactly what is being required,
they usually commit wholeheartedly to the activity, making melodrama look mild in the process.

Exercise 66: GIBBERISH
Gibberish, that is, speaking nonsense with familiar inflections, can be a most liberating tool for young actors. In one exercise, we have our students pair up and
begin improvising some dialogue in character. At a certain
point, we tell them to switch into gibberish, but all the while
continuing the thread of their conversation. Then, at frequent, irregular intervals, we have them bounce back and
forth between English and gibberish. Whenever we have
employed this activity, we have nearly always made the

same objective observation—unfailingly, the energy level and volume in the room rises dramatically when the students speak gibberish, then dwindles back to normal during the English exchanges.

A far more ambitious variation is the GIBBERISH TRANSLATION exercise. Again pair actors up, and have one of them think of some activity to perform in front of an audience: demonstrating how to prepare some esoteric recipe, selling some new-fangled product, giving testimony at a hearing before a Congressional panel. Then the actor launches into his or her presentation, only in gibberish, complete with accompanying gestures. After a sentence or two, call upon the presenter's "interpreter" to translate the gibberish into understandable English. Of course, the interpreter has no idea what the presenter is really saying (just as often, neither does the presenter), so it falls to the interpreter to improvise the translation, based at least somewhat upon the tone of the presenter's voice and the quality of the gestures. Here is a silly example:

> Presenter, holding an imaginary gadget: Drpez ini
> orfnok—lalaeatchno mo lorni fobga
> eolkabus.

> Interpreter: Now you can own this astonishing
> new patented device—a titanium-sheathed,
> computer-engineered, gamma ray Gnome
> Sighter!

> Presenter: Olbul nis ek minorik shlub fa sar icknori
> blu aragober, ul megor rebos wana soog
> alt boorinog?

> Interpreter: How many times have you wished you
> could see those mischievous little beings who
> put your car keys in different locations than

where you put them down, or who pinch all those socks that disappear from the dryer?

Presenter: Belesh sko nelu ig noria flascumok ilian blogopi homique terranovsh el fromicar retyr joflanic pertopow zedu namiva trimolk werty ip hojrex pitwin axorinda plusca putberty nof itvicorus ascogia trug filianor mosi li alfo.

Interpreter: With this ingenius device you will be able to train your sights on even the most crafty of gnomes by using the technological breakthrough that recognizes and digitally reproduces any gnome's aura.

Presenter: Tramilio boxu oriepro freenul. Ag mool!

Interpreter: So let the remarkable Gnome de Plume help you find those pesky tricksters. All you have to do is send in $12.99 and your first born to qualify for this one-time offer. Hurry!

Exercise 67: ONE KNOWS, ONE DOESN'T

Ask two actors to volunteer for a scene. Whisper to one who she is and what the context is; the other person plays the scene "blind," groping to figure out who he is based on the gradually unfolding clues of his partner. Imagine that the actor in the know is told she is a painter, and her partner in the dark is a restless model.

Painter: (Perhaps in a French accent) Stop moving so much.

Actor #2: I can't help it. I have mosquito bites all over my body.

Painter: That's why I asked you to keep your outfit on.

Actor #2: (still uncertain who he is playing and what his relationship to the "painter" is, but clearly interested in the possibilities of the last remark) Don't you want to play Adam and Eve?

Painter: I'm much more interested in capturing the interplay of light on fabric than in seeing swollen red blotches. Now please remain still!

Actor #2: (beginning to get the context) Must I continue to balance on one leg?

Painter: And up on tiptoe!

Actor #2: (Now relishing his newly discovered direction) My tutu is too tight. I have no feeling in my extremities.

Painter: That's what happens when you squeeze a size 48 body into a size 6 tights!

Actor #2: Oh well, I suppose losing a limb is a small price to pay for the sake of art!

The key to such improvs is how artfully, and subtly the informed actor reveals the situation to his or her ignorant partner. If, in the above scene, the painter had begun with, "How do you expect me to capture on canvas your classic ballet pose with your wriggling about?", the discovery process would have been entirely short-circuited, and the actors' and audience's interest would have instantly evaporated. Dropping general clues (especially those that offer wide-open possibilities for misinterpretation, at least in the beginning) and proceeding to more specific and orienting hints make for most absorbing theater.

Situations for such scenes are limitless but might include the following:

— a lawyer speaking to his prisoner/client
— veterinarian speaking to pet owner
— a bus driver to an unruly kid in the back
— an eighty-five-year-old husband informing his wife of 60 years that he's leaving her for a younger woman
— expectant fathers in a waiting room
— an environmentalist confronting a logger
— a boss to a secretary who has just ruined the copier
— a homeowner interrupting a bungling burglar
— two gravediggers in Brooklyn
— astronauts about to take off

Exercise 68: GIFT-GIVING
In the previous exercise, at least one player knows the situation and can guide his or her partner in the intended direction. However, this exercise removes all such directional aids. Neither participant begins with even the slightest hint where the scene is going. Ask one actor to hand another an imaginary package; other than communicating the general size and weight of the package, there's no way of knowing the contents until the recipient unwraps the present. In fact, neither actor has any idea what the gift is. They both must discover it through the ensuing improvised scene:

Receiver: Oh, my gosh! How did you know that I've been coveting this for years?

Giver: I'm psychic.

Receiver: Who told you? Andrea? Millie? Rex?

Giver: I'm not revealing my sources. Do you really like it?

Receiver: Like it? I adore it! But do you think it's too . . . you know . . . bold?

Giver: How can we know until you try it on?

(This is the first real stab at narrowing down the possibilities. They now know they're dealing with some apparel, and not with a CD or a fishing rod. The recipient now must take a leap of imagination, reach into the box and let his hands create some item of clothing. He places an invisible hat on his head).

Giver: It's perfect! You were born to wear it.

(Up to this point neither participant knows yet what kind of hat they are describing. One or the other actor has to offer a direction).

Recipient: I feel so . . . wild and woodsy with it on.

Giver: All you need now is one of those fringed buckskin shirts and a musket.

(Clearly the giver has taken the recipient's suggestion further, "seen" exactly what kind of hat the recipient is wearing and has also given her partner all the direction he needs to complete the scene).

Recipient: But should I wear it with the tail in the back or the front?

Again, the real challenge in playing such improvisations is to allow the discovery process to unfold slowly (much more slowly than the illustration above has indicated), instead of trying to rush into some fixed and finished solution. It is precisely that unresolved groping in which audiences find such delight. Onstage, questions are so much more interesting than answers. A student of mine put it even more aptly in an American literature course I was teaching a few years ago. I asked the students to come up with some original thought, or at least one for which they could find no antecedent. This young man wrote, "Questions are better than answers, for answers are just questions cut short by arrogance." An exercise such as GIFT-GIVING encourages the humility that only living questions can engender.

Exercise 69: WHAT'S IN THE CLOSET?
Similar to GIFT-GIVING, this exercise begins with both actors in complete ignorance of their scene's direction. Direct one of them to go to an imaginary closet door, open it and then say something along the lines of, "Would you please tell me what this is doing in here?"
Depending on the first actor's tone of voice and general reaction, the second actor can advance the conversation with some new information: "Where else am I going to keep it? You already told me that it would be dangerous to keep it in the bedroom!" Again, young actors should fight the urge to pin down the identification of the closeted item for a while. Let the tension build that can arise out of this ensemble groping towards a joint imagination.

Exercise 70: RHYMING DIALOGUE
The trend in modern poetry has been to disdain rhyme schemes, with good reason. Unless it is deftly done, rhyming can quickly fall into a predictable, sing-song tempo that detracts from, rather than augments, a poem's content.

Yet in an improvisational context, asking actors to transform otherwise prose dialogue into rhyme can have the most electrifying effects. Perhaps you can initiate this exercise by giving your instructions in rhyme.

> All right, everybody, look lively, it's time
>   for all you actors to speak in rhyme.
> Whatever lines you have you must find a way
>   for the last words to rhyme, now heed what I say,
>   no matter if you're clothed in burlap, rayon, lace
>   or doublet,
>   either rhyme alternatingly or in your standard
>   couplet!

Not exactly Shakespearean in quality, but that's precisely the point. The clumsier your rhyming, the less daunting and more empowering the challenge will be for the actors. While you can use this activity for any improvisational work, it can be particularly effective towards the end of a production. If your actors have fallen into patterned ways of speaking their lines, bordering on the mechanical, or if they have stopped listening to one another, spring this exercise on them to shake them out of their lockstep. Have them enact a scene from the play, but now roughly translating their lines from the original into rhyme. Cornelius, in Thornton Wilder's *The Matchmaker*, addresses the audience with the following speech:

Isn't the world full of wonderful things? There we sit cooped up in Yonkers years and years and years and all the time wonderful people like Mrs. Molloy are walking around in New York and we don't know them at all. I don't know whether—from where you're sitting—you can see—well, for instance, the way her eye and cheek come together, up here. Can you? And the kind of fireworks that shoot out of her eyes all the time. I tell you right now; a fine woman is the greatest work of God.

(Act II, p. 176)

Such a speech might be versified in the following manner:

Isn't the world full of wonder and joy?
    We sit in Yonkers for years and never know
    that people exist like Mrs. Molloy.
    Can you see from where you sit, just so,
    how her cheek and eye and temple meet
    to form this irresistible line?
    How her eyes shoot—now isn't this neat—
    sparklers and fireworks the entire time?

    I tell you all now that with all a woman's features
    God's never created more enchanting creatures.

Another variation of this exercise is to have two characters improvise some dialogue—perhaps inspired by a scene in the play—in which one actor speaks a line ending with a word that can be rhymed. Then the other must speak the next line ending with a matching rhyming word.

    Cornelius: Chief clerk! Oh Boy! I've been promoted from chief clerk to chief clerk.

    Barnaby: Aren't you happy? You're finally getting somewhere in your work.

    Cornelius: I don't want to work every day of the week. I want to live!

    Barnaby: Oh, it's not so bad, Cornelius; it beats being a sieve.

    Cornelius: Barnaby, how much money have you got?

    Barnaby: Three dollars—hey, that's a lot!

Cornelius: We're going to New York to paint the town red!

Barnaby: We can't, Cornelius, by nine I'm in bed.

Cornelius: Don't you want some excitement in your life?

Barnaby: I have quite enough whittling with my penknife.

Cornelius: Well, I'm 33 and I've never kissed a girl, you see?

Barnaby: Yes, but I'm only 17; it's not so urgent for me!

Exercise 71: CHARACTER EXCHANGE

Involve two actors in an improvised dialogue of some kind. The scene could arise from some moment peripherally related to or suggested by, but not actually dramatized in, the play which you are working. *In Much Ado About Nothing*, it might be the first time Beatrice and Benedick ever verbally sparred with one another. In *Under Milkwood*, it could be Polly Garter's visiting Captain Cat on his deathbed. If you are not working with a formal play, the scene could be purely fabricated from any situation that might involve the clash of two very different perspectives, such as one of the following:

— a student being called into the principal's office
— a psychic breaking some bad future news to a client
— a city dweller arguing with a farmer about the merits of urban vs. country life
— a rude customer and an irritable shop owner

— a policeman stopping a speeding motorist
— two inventors of the same device trying to take sole credit
— a barber and the customer whose hair he just butchered
— a conductor to an incompetent oboist in the orchestra

Allow the conversation to develop so that the participants establish their respective views. Then, at a moment when the dialogue begins to heat up, freeze the action. While holding the freeze, have each person note carefully the other's physical position—the tilt of the head, the location of the hands, the attitude of the legs and feet. At the director's signal, the actors change places, meticulously replicating their partner's position as precisely as possible. Each actor holds this new pose until the director says, "Continue," whereupon the actors now carry on with the scene assuming the identity of the person with whom they were just arguing. The actors now must, initially at least, maintain the original view advanced by their partners. At other critical junctures, the pair can exchange places again and again, until a suitable endpoint is reached.

This exercise can be particularly effective for an actor who latches on to one particular interpretation and then defends it rigidly against all constructive suggestions. Beyond that, it is one of the most effective vehicles for broadening young people's awareness, so that they see beyond their own, fairly narrow standpoints. One of the great stumbling blocks to ensemble playing in the theater, and for that matter to real community building in the world, is our inability to value another person's point of view. Sometimes we can only come to such a recognition when life circumstances compel us to walk in another's shoes. A drama exercise such as CHARACTER EXCHANGE can help to develop the expanded awareness necessary for us to acknowledge and appreciate differences.

PART THREE

PRACTICAL ASPECTS OF MOUNTING A PRODUCTION

Chapter XI

Finding the Right Play

I once asked a well-known poet about his inspiration for writing. He replied, "Every so often I get a feeling like a chicken bone is stuck in my throat. That's when I know I've got a poem coming. It's those chicken bones that turn into poems." What is the "chicken bone" that provokes a dramatic production? One cannot say that the empty stage, as Peter Brooke termed it, calls forth a play any more insistently than the poet's blank sheet of paper does, or the painter's untouched canvas. For the teacher/director, the starting point must be the group of eager young actors who need a particular kind of dramatic experience. Beginning with a specific play in mind, and then gathering a group of actors to mount the production, may work in professional or community theater. Such an approach in a school setting overlooks the primary reason for doing a play in the first place— the needs of the students.

How does one choose a play to meet those needs? Can the director know a class well enough to judge whether it needs the levity and verbal acrobatics of a witty Molière comedy or the deepening intensity of a Greek tragedy? When can Shakespeare be tackled? Where can one find modern plays filled with idealism instead of cynicism?

In an ideal world, of course, the teacher would write a class play each year on an age-appropriate theme. One of my gifted colleagues has done just that, including a recently staged adaptation of *Parzival* for his seventh graders. Writing one's own script allows the teacher to customize every student's role. The loudmouth needing to be sensitive to others may be given the part of a mute; the taciturn girl in the corner may benefit from playing a tart-tongued shrew; the child who lacks will might become a courageous warrior. Such are the possibilities when one can compose the play one directs.

Not all of us are both literary and dramatic, so to find a suitable play we must rely on the works of other authors. What is suitable? In the Waldorf world, the curriculum can offer a most helpful direction. For example, seventh graders study the Middle Ages, the Renaissance, and the Age of Exploration. Many classes have performed one version or another of Joan of Arc's life; last year the seventh graders at my school turned three of Chaucer's *Canterbury Tales* into a delightful evening of theater. Then eighth grade students are introduced to the modern world by way of the American, French, and Industrial Revolutions. Plays about Lincoln, adaptations of Dickens' stories, such as *A Tale of Two Cities or Nicholas Nickleby*, Lawrence and Lee's *The Night Thoreau Spent in Jail*, Rostand's *Cyrano de Bergerac*, and the musical *Fiddler on the Roof* have all offered worthwhile themes for eighth graders.

Other considerations besides curricular themes may need to be weighed when choosing a play. In tenth grade, for example, our students find themselves exploring ancient civilizations, from India to Greece. While it is possible to stage some exceedingly distilled version of the *Mahabharata* (Peter Brooke's ground-breaking adaptation in the late eighties was over nine hours long), one of the classic Greek plays might be a more manageable choice. Indeed, with a small class of students, *Antigone* or

Prometheus Bound could work well. The Greek canon of tragedies contains some of the most unadorned, powerful, poignant depictions of the human condition ever written. The biggest practical problem with these otherwise potent dramas is the lack of leading roles. Antigone only offers a director five or six major characters to work with; the rest of the class would have to be content with being members of the all-important chorus. Over the years, however, I have come to realize that such choral work, while challenging, does not always meet the needs of rapidly incarnating adolescents who hunger to play individuals. Being part of a strong chorus that speaks and moves in graceful unison seems more appropriate to fifth graders. They still live much more strongly in a group consciousness. So for our sophomore productions, we have turned to playwrights who provide young actors with three essential ingredients:

1) **Strong characterizations**—real individuals who are complicated enough to allow students to discover hidden dimensions, subterranean motives, and a range of emotions

2) **Rich language**—that in the speaking can actually transport young actors to a level they might not otherwise reach using mundane, everyday speech. Language, as Orwell so presciently pointed out in *1984*, diminishes or elevates consciousness according to the variety, color, and texture of possible word choices. Finding a play with such rich language can actually ennoble the speakers and expand not only their vocabulary, but also their sense of themselves

3) **Stirring storylines**—a narrative that grips the imagination, one that has transformative possibilities for the characters and the actors who play them. We look for a play that dramatizes familiar, yet universal themes of

striving after the ideals that make us human—love, beauty, truth, redemption, sacrifice, courage, forgiveness. Perhaps it is no wonder that so many directors turn to the one playwright who managed four hundred years ago to encompass each of these elements into his time-transcending explorations of the human condition—William Shakespeare.

Playing Shakespeare

> If it be not now, yet it will come. Readiness is all.
> (*Hamlet*, Act V, scene ii)

Not a single class has graduated from Green Meadow Waldorf School in the last twelve years without having had the opportunity to perform a Shakespeare play. The only small controversy over the years has been not *whether* to undertake a Shakespeare play, but *when*. So many Waldorf schools without high schools view performing Shakespeare as a culminating challenge of students' entire elementary school experience. If, in fact, the eighth grade is the last chance for students to do Shakespeare, then by all means, forge ahead. Yet we have discovered at least a couple of good reasons for waiting until tenth or eleventh grade to tackle Shakespeare.

I have seen a number of eighth-grade productions of various Shakespeare comedies. On one level or another, of course, they have all been delightful, especially if one knows the students who revel in portraying a sodden Sir Toby Belch or a jackass-enamored Titania or tart-tongued adversaries such as Kate and Petruchio. Yet from another perspective, most eighth graders seem somewhat overmatched playing Shakespeare. They often do not understand and, therefore, cannot fully ensoul the majestic language they are declaiming. At the same time, they are rarely capable of bringing enough depth and dimension to these memorable individualities. Falstaff and Feste, Portia and

Prospero, Iago and Ophelia, Benedick and Beatrice—these and dozens of larger-than-life characters have often become career-making (or -breaking) roles for professional actors. For young teenagers just beginning to experience the first seething storms of their own inner realms, it may be a bit premature to immerse them in Shakespeare.

The same might be said, of course, for a sixteen- or seventeen-year-old. Yet any teacher of adolescents will confirm the enormous deepening of young people's capacities in the interval of those two or three years. In the Waldorf school movement which distinguishes itself from other educational models through its age-appropriate curriculum, this is no small matter. Suddenly, the jealous rage of a Leontes or Othello, the overweening, ruthless ambitions of a Lady Macbeth, and the paralyzing self-loathing of a Hamlet no longer seem out of the reach of a talented young actor. Simply put, older teenagers have more emotional cache to call upon than younger adolescents, more gathering ego strength to anchor their characters and to subdue their own personal tempests than fourteen-year-olds. None of this is to say that elementary school students should not stage a Shakespeare play; only that, given the choice, older students will bring more to, and receive more from, the treasures of a Shakespeare production than younger actors.

Some Shakespeare-worshiping teachers might object by countering that students can never be exposed enough to the bard's genius. As early as first and second grades, some children skip around the room reciting Ariel's "Come unto these yellow sands" song, and few seventh graders escape the first serious exploration of poetry without learning a Shakespearean sonnet or two. At the right time, such introductions can only be enriching. The only caution here is not to fall into the thought-trap of mainstream education. The prevailing philosophy assumes that if reading is important to learn, and tests are the best way to ascertain what students learn, then the earlier that reading can be taught and tests administered, the better. If we were to follow that approach to its illogical extreme, parents wishing to raise future Olympic champions might start three-year-olds on weight-lifting regimes; more cerebral parents, already grooming their child for that doctoral thesis, might replace their five-year-old's bedtime fairy tales with a steady diet of Great Books authors—Plato, Thomas Aquinas, Descartes, Darwin. Just as children who, at the urging of ambitious parents, begin competitive sports too early and burn out by the time they hit adolescence, so, too, students exposed too early or too intensely to Shakespeare may resist the bard's gifts later in life.

Chapter XII

Cut to the Quick—
Even Shakespeare Needed an Editor

Only a dramatic genius such as Shakespeare could give Polonius, that old windbag of a counselor in *Hamlet*, some of the most perceptive words ever spoken on a stage, or for the stage:

> Since brevity is the soul of wit . . .
> I will be brief.
> (Act II, scene ii)

The joke, of course, is that Polonius speaks these lines just as he is warming up for a speech so interminable that it becomes a parody of every convoluted explanation ever delivered. Polonius has a knack for turning a simple sentence into a voluminous commentary. Is it heresy to suggest that Shakespeare himself was guilty of the same prolixity, at least when one considers staging one of his plays with young actors? This may sound contradictory to the statement above alluding to Shakespeare's majestic language. Yet as vital and time-transcending as his verse has proven over the centuries, mounting a Shakespeare play without prudent editing would be hard on both actors and audience.

Perhaps we should not fault Shakespeare; perhaps the blame lies with us. How many of us have allowed our consciousness to be whittled away and hollowed out by media, until we have trouble focusing on any experience that exceeds the twelve-minute attention span between television commericals? How many of us latch onto one convenient, empty-headed advertising sound byte or another, such as "Just do it," or "Is it in you?" or "Like a rock"? Is it so surprising that most adolescents' favorite all-purpose word of the moment is the pithy, noncommittal "Whatever"?

Whatever the reason, even a brilliantly directed Shakespeare play needs editing if young actors are performing it. Indeed, with the time constraints most teacher/directors have to endure, a shortened version of the play in question becomes not just desirable, but imperative. So how can a decidedly nongenius teacher/director presume to wield the scalpel that excises a third or more of *Twelfth Night* or *Macbeth* or *As You Like It*? For teachers unaccustomed to such "tailoring," the idea must sound tantamount to only playing two of every three notes of a Beethoven concerto, or looking only at the lines, and not the colors, of a Cezanne painting. Nevertheless, it is possible to artfully edit Shakespeare's work without anyone in the audience, outside of a few Shakespearean scholars, knowing what has been snipped.

Would-be editors must first take the time to familiarize themselves with the play in question—not just by reading it through, but by studying it thoroughly, looking for imagery, themes, and references in early scenes that appear in later ones. After a number of close readings, they should take a pencil and lightly bracket any line, any exchange between characters, any seemingly redundant passage in a longer speech, that might be eliminated without losing the storyline or mood of the scene. Here is an example from *Twelfth Night*:

Enter Maria and Clown

[Lines to be deleted appear in boldface.]

Mar: Nay, either tell me where thou hast been,
   or I will not open my lips so wide as a bristle may
   enter in way of thy excuse. My lady will hang thee
   for thy absence.

Clown: Let her hang me! He that is well hanged
   in this world needs to fear no colors.

Mar: Make that good.

Clown: He shall see none to fear.

Mar: A good lenten answer. I can tell thee where
   that saying was born, of "I fear no colors."

Clown: Where, good Mistress Mary?

Mar: In the wars; and that may you be bold to say
   in your foolery.

Clown: Well, God give them wisdom that have it;
   and those that are fools, let them use their talents.

Mar: Yet you will be hanged for being so long absent,
   or to be turned away—is not that as good as a hanging to you?

Clown: Many a good hanging prevents a bad marriage; and for turning away, let summer bear it out.

Mar: You are resolute then?

Clown: Not so, neither; but I am resolved on two
   points.

Mar: That if one break, the other will hold; or if
both break, your gaskins fall.

Clown: Apt, in good faith; very apt. Well go thy way!
If Sir Toby would leave drinking, thou wert as witty
a piece of flesh as any in Illyria.

Mar: Peace, you rogue; no more o' that. Here comes
my lady. Make your excuse wisely, you were best.
(Act I, scene v)

This brief exchange cannot be excised completely
without losing two key elements: 1) examples of both
Maria's and the Clown's trenchant wit, and 2) the fore-
shadowing in the Clown's final lines of Sir Toby's eventual
coupling with Maria. At the same time, the more obscure
references in the exchange can be omitted without losing
the lifeblood of the characters' dialogue. We must be extremely careful, of course, not to be so rash and indiscrimi-
nate in editing such scenes that we "sever an artery" or
"remove a vital organ." Furthermore, whatever lines we
excise, we must stitch the remaining text back together as
seamlessly as possible. This can only be achieved by making sure that the dialogue on either side of a cut betrays no
hint of excision, as the example above illustrates. If we can
learn to become artistic surgeons, the resulting abridge-
ments of Shakespeare's plays will be true to his own creative impulses. Indeed, many of Shakespeare's greatest
stories were lifted from other sources, then truncated, re-
cast, embellished, and transformed by the bard himself.

Prudent paring should not be limited to
Shakespeare. By the end of their secondary school careers,
most twelfth graders long to perform a contemporary play,
one that has, in the words of a recent senior, "everything—
levity and gravity, a gripping story, juicy characters,
meaningful theme." They don't ask for much, do they?

The obvious problem for large high school classes (greater than twenty or twenty-five) is that the trend in the most memorable twentieth-century drama has been towards smaller and smaller casts: Eugene O'Neill's *Long Day's Journey into Night* has five parts; so do Samuel Beckett's *Waiting for Godot,* John Osborne's *Look Back in Anger,* and Edward Albee's *The American Dream.* Harold Pinter's *The Birthday Party* has six roles, Frances Goodrich's and Albert Hackett's *The Diary of Ann Frank* offers ten, William Inge's *Picnic,* eleven. Of course, one can find notable exceptions—Wilder's plays, Miller's *The Crucible,* and Moss and Hart's comedies; and we have turned to these playwrights more than once over the years. (See Chapter XVIII: "Plays That Have Worked" for a list of larger-cast plays we have done with some success.)

The other problem has more to do with the content of contemporary drama. As the world has turned darker, many playwrights have naturally chosen to dramatize the growing violence, cynicism, and alienation of our time. One could argue, of course, that few modern plays rival *Hamlet* for exposing the depravity, the estrangement, the shadow side of the human soul. For sheer iniquity, what other play boasts a father's ghost who demands bloody revenge for his "unnatural murder," a mother who marries the murderer, lifelong friends who turn into spies, a young woman who goes insane and essentially commits suicide after hearing about her father's death at the hands of her would-be lover, and no fewer than seven other deaths during the story—death by drowning, venom, execution, swordpoint? What could be darker than the final scene? The treachery that has literally poisoned the world of Elsinore has left the stage littered with corpses.

And yet, through it all, we have witnessed the imperishable nobility of an individual struggling to find truth, love, and meaning in a wicked world. The magnitude of Hamlet's questioning, the immensity of his soul, elevates the play into the highest reaches of human striving. Yes, *Hamlet* is a tragedy, but because it is, we experience all the *eleos* and *phobos*—the compassion and awe—Aristotle described over twenty-five hundred years ago. In tragedy we see the human spirit laid bare, and it is an awe-inspiring, humbling sight. Real tragedy is not paralyzing or dispiriting; it transmutes pain into illumination. Through tragedy, we discover the depths as well as the heights of what it means to be truly human.

Many contemporary plays lack precisely this transcendent, revelatory quality, precisely because they deny the power of the human spirit. The theatrical adaptation of Orwell's *1984* is a perfect example of this crushing, dehumanizing trend. Winston Smith is more a victim than a tragic figure, whose physical and psychological torture, whose ultimate self-surrender to Big Brother at the story's end, offers no hint of nobility, no crumb of hope, no whisper of redemption. One can certainly claim that dramatizing visions of such dystopias can serve as a warning to all who scoff at the notion of such a brutal totalitarian state. Yet ever again we educators/directors need to ask ourselves what soul nourishment can a particular play provide young people who are looking to find their moral bearings in the murky currents of our uncertain world.

Two of the most inspirational modern plays I have worked with are Dylan Thomas' *Under Milkwood* and Frank Galati's adaptation of Steinbeck's *The Grapes of Wrath*. *Under Milkwood* is Thomas' loving, twenty-four hour depiction of Welsh fishing village denizens. It contains dozens of all-too-human and memorable characters, in addition to some of the richest, most poetic language of the twentieth century. *The Grapes of Wrath*, as described elsewhere, dramatizes the dreams, the despair, the simple dignity, and the innate goodness of the Joad family as they encounter tragedy and injustice in their move from Oklahoma's dust bowl to California's fruit-growing fields. Although both plays are beautifully written, again I edited and spliced to suit our needs.

With *The Grapes of Wrath*, time constraints again dictated a number of abbreviated scenes, such as the one below:

[Lines to be deleted appear in boldface.]

Casy: I been thinkin'. I been in the hills thinkin', almost you might say like Jesus went into the wilderness to think His way out of a mess of troubles.

Granma: Pu-raise Gawd!

Casy: I ain't sayin' I'm like Jesus. But I got tired like Him, an' I got mixed up like Him, an' I went into the wilderness like Him, without no campin' stuff.

Granma: Hallelujah!

Casy: I been thinkin', on'y it wasn't thinkin', it was deeper down than thinkin'. I got thinkin' how there was the moon an' the stars an' the hills, an' there was me lookin' at 'em, an' we wasn't separate no more. We was one thing. An' that one thing was holy.

I got thinkin' how **we was holy when we was one thing, an'** mankin' was holy when it was one thing. **An' it on'y got unholy when one mis-able little fella got the bit in his teeth an' run off his own way, kickin' an' draggin' an' fightin'. Fella like that bust the holiness. But when they're all workin' together—kind of harnessed to the whole shebang—that's right, that's holy.** An' then I got thinkin' I don't even know what I mean by holy. I can't say no grace like I use' ta say. I'm glad of the holiness of supper. I'm glad there's love here. That's all. (Heads remain bowed. Casy looks around.) I've got your supper cold. Amen.

All: A-men.

(Act I, pp. 24-25)

With *Under Milkwood*, I wanted to reduce some of the narration to give more playing time to the character-revealing vignettes. An example follows:

[Lines to be deleted appear in boldface.]

Organ Morgan: There is perturbation and music in Coronation Street! All the spouses are honking like geese and the babies singing opera. **P. C. Attila Rees has got his truncheon out and is playing cadenzas by the pump, the cows from Sunday Meadow ring like reindeer, and on the roof of Handel Villa see the Women's Welfare hoofing, bloomered, in the moon.**

First Voice: **At the sea-end of town, Mr. and Mrs. Floyd, the cocklers, are sleeping as quiet as death, side by wrinkled side, toothless, salt and brown like two old kippers in a box.**
    And high above, in Salt Lake Farm, Mr. Utah Watkins counts, all night, the wife-faced sheep as they leap the fences on the hill, smiling and knitting and bleating just like Mrs. Utah Watkins.

Utah Watkins: Thirty-four, thirty-five, thirty-six, forty-eight, eighty-nine . . .

Mrs. Utah Watkins: (bleating) Knit one slip one
                                 Knit two together
                                 Pass the slipstitch over

First Voice: Ocky Milkman, drowned asleep in Cockle Street, is emptying his churns into the Dewi River,

140

Ocky Milkman: (whispering) regardless of expense,

First Voice: and weeping like a funeral.

Second Voice: Cherry Own, next door, lifts a tankard to his lips, but nothing flows out of it. He shakes the tankard. It turns into a fish. He drinks the fish.

First Voice: P. C. Attila Rees lumps out of bed, dead to the dark and still foghorning, and drags out his helmet from under the bed; but deep in the back yard lock-up of his sleep a mean voice murmurs.

A Voice: You'll be sorry for this in the morning,

First Voice: and he heave-ho's back to bed. His helmet swashes in the dark.

Second Voice: Willy Nilly, postman, asleep up street, walks fourteen miles to deliver the post as he does every day of the night, and rat-a-tats hard and sharp on Mrs. Willy Nilly.

Mrs. Willy Nilly: Don't spank me, please, teacher,

Second Voice: whimpers his wife at his side, but every night of her married life she has been late for school.

(pp. 18-20)

The hardest part of trimming any play, of course, is knowing that for the playwright, every line is a vital strand in the play's tapestry; cutting any single strand could cause the fabric to unravel. In a play such as *Under Milkwood*, we language-loving directors could well cringe at our own audacity when taking the knife to Thomas' incomparably lyrical lines. Nevertheless, we need to remind ourselves that we are not working with professional actors, nor do we have an open-ended calendar. Given the choice of performing badly a full-length, unabridged production or performing well a discriminatingly edited play, who would knowingly choose the agony over the ecstasy?

As a final word on editing, I should issue a note of caution: any editing a person does without permission from either the playwright or publishing company is probably breaking one law or another. The same is true for reproducing scripts on copiers and performing plays without paying required royalty fees. That said, I know of very few theatrical productions at the junior high or high school level that are not altered in some way to suit the specific needs of a particular class or community.

Scene from The Matchmaker – *10th grade production*

Chapter XIII

Casting the Play

There are no small roles—only small actors.

Anonymous

In the Waldorf school world, teachers carry within them a constant, but usually unspoken, commission. They strive to envision the higher self of each child entrusted to their care. This imagining can be therapeutic for both teacher and student; for the former, it can serve as a reminder that a child's misbehavior on any given day is just a shadow cast by a greater light. For the latter, a teacher's meditative thoughts can have the most profound and salutary effects upon the child. Perhaps in some mysterious way they provide the child with a guiding image for his or her future. A teacher's vividly pictured imaginations may act as "invisible cairns"—those small piles of rocks that hikers follow to mark a trail above the timberline. Graduates who come back to alumni events years later sometimes comment about these signposts. "When I was in the Waldorf school," said one alumna at a recent gathering, "I felt as if the teachers knew me better than I knew myself. I felt cared for and carried through hard times."

At no time is this picturing of the child more pertinent than when it comes time to cast a play. Yet it is precisely at this point in the production that we teachers, who are also the directors, can encounter an apparent conflict of interests. Any teacher/director with pedagogical intentions handles the process of casting with the utmost sensitivity. What role would best serve the present and future needs of each child? Does one cast with or against type? Should the class jester be given the part of the clown or the role of a taciturn hermit? Will the painfully shy child be overwhelmed by, or rise to, the challenge of playing the leading character? Will it be more therapeutic for the class' most self-absorbed young fellow to be given an attention-getting part or the minor role of a self-effacing monk?

At the same time, as directors of adolescents, we must balance pedagogical considerations against the artistic requirements of the play. If we think only in terms of individual children's needs, the quality of the performances may suffer irreparable harm. Assigning to a young person a major role far beyond his or her capacities is not pedagogical; it is cruel and unusual punishment, both for the individual and the other actors who want their play to be as good as it can be. In actuality, there should be no conflict between pedagogical and artistic objectives; if a play is an artistic triumph, it will also have pedagogical value. However, a play hopelessly mangled by ill-chosen casting may not be just an artistic fiasco; it will have pedagogical implications as well. Young people need to experience success in their artistic collaborations. Certainly, one can point to the character-building aspects of failure. But the athletic field seems to be a better venue than the stage for such life lessons. Presumably a teacher/director has more control of a production's success or failure than a coach has over winning or losing some baseball game.

What constitutes success, theatrically speaking, in our Waldorf circles, or, for that matter, in any amateur setting? We have no commercial gauge—no scathing or flattering drama reviews in the local paper, no months-in-advance reserved seating or standing room audiences, no speculators clamoring to underwrite our next venture. For me the criteria for success can be reduced to two questions: 1) Did the actors grow from the challenge of mounting the production? 2) Was the audience moved on some level by seeing the play?

If young people's growth is one of the primary aims of dramatic work, then the ideal casting process will offer appropriate acting challenges for the maximum number of students. Given the general shortage of juicy roles in most plays, we have resorted to double-casting many of our recent productions, that is, giving the same part to two different individuals. This method presents some inherent risks, but the advantages outweigh the drawbacks. Most critics of double-casting believe that it fosters competitiveness and inevitable comparisons between young actors. "Oh, Marcie was much better than Sarah as Helen Keller—Sarah just wasn't as expressive or as believable." However, students can be positioned to work collaboratively on the same role. They can work on lines together, build the character together by sharing their differing perspectives. Each can borrow nuances, gestures, and inflections from the other. On a more pragmatic level, having two people prepare for the same role virtually eliminates anxiety over an actor's last-minute illness. Two years ago, just days before a performance of *A Winter's Tale*, one of our leads contracted acute bronchitis and a high fever. Fortunately, we had double-cast the part, and the other Paulina was already prepared to fill in admirably.

One practical difficulty is the added time necessary to rehearse with two actors playing the same role. A possible way of mitigating this time pressure is to block the play with both actors onstage, speaking their lines simultaneously. Another possibility is to ask one actor to shadow the other in the early phases of production, so both players are familiar with entrances, exits, crosses. Cramming a doubled cast into the playing area can certainly clutter the stage initially, but your playing area will seem downright capacious, once rehearsals involve only one cast at a time.

However, any double-cast actors not onstage at the time must be present and alert to all directions, so that when they get an opportunity to rehearse, the director need not waste time repeating him/herself.

Double-casting offers yet another benefit—as a remedy for the tendency towards staleness or rote portrayals in a production. Some professional companies have long recognized this; to keep their principal actors fresh, they have them alternate roles from week to week, or even from performance to performance. Imagine the challenge of playing Othello one night and Iago the next! What depth of understanding and inner mobility the actors must bring to both roles. Double-casting at the junior high or high school level can have a similarly stimulating effect for the entire production. No two interpretations of a role are ever the same.

Never was this more apparent than in a recent sophomore production of Wilder's *The Matchmaker*. I had cast two extraordinarily different girls in the leading role. One was stout, sunny, immediately capable of expressing Dolly Levi's brassy manner. From the outset, she manufactured a marvelous Brooklyn accent. Her counterpart was tall, willowy, a bit more muted vocally but very expressive physically. She conveyed more of Dolly's subtler, scheming side with inflections and gestures reminiscent of a young Mae West. Both these actresses brought their own distinctive gifts to the play, and both gave sparkling performances. It was a pleasure to see them working together; without a doubt, their collaboration helped each one develop qualities the other naturally possessed. Ideally, however, double-casting might be limited to less central parts, or at least to roles whose characters are in fewer scenes, to reduce duplication during rehearsals.

As for actually assigning parts, I am not averse to enlisting the ideas of the teenagers themselves. Asking the actors to cast the play can be very helpful, as long as they realize that their lists can only be considered suggestions and not ironclad guarantees. With high school students, I usually ask them to cast their classmates in roles most advantageous to the play as a whole, and then to include three parts that they themselves would not object to playing: one large, one medium-sized, and one smaller role. Generally, I try to accommodate their wishes if I sense that they have chosen parts with the greater good of the production in mind. However, some overly ambitious students have occasionally resorted to lobbying, in an attempt to influence their classmates' casting decisions. An unexpected groundswell of support for someone on the casting lists might tip off the director to such overly enthusiastic lobbying.

Chapter XIV

The Production Schedule

Luck is the residue of design.
                                    Branch Rickey

In one's personal life, being organized or living
with chaos is largely a matter of temperament or choice. In
a theatrical production, organization and foresight are less
a matter of choice than of necessity. Woe to the director
who thinks he or she can pull together a play without proper
planning. A hundred and one details, both onstage and
behind the scenes, must be taken into account before the
fact, or they will explode like little land mines on the set.
Forgot to order the muslin for the flats? It might take ten
precious days to receive it, more if it has to be back ordered.
Did you reserve the hall for that extra Saturday rehearsal,
or will you be sharing the space with the local aerobics class?
Did you make sure safety pins were on hand for the dress
rehearsal? Did you remember the penlight for the prompter,
the music for the pianist, the suspenders for the character
playing Grandpa, the electric tape to hide the lighting wires?
Did you forget to thank Millie in the program for all her
work with costumes, and Mr. Johnson for helping to trans-

form a rolling television cart into an Okie truck? For that matter, did you forget about the programs altogether?

Directors need to think through, in advance, every phase of a production. A lighting design cannot really be tackled until a set design is completed. A choreographer will have a hard time creating a dance unless the music and available stage space are identified first. How can a costuming crew begin work without a color scheme and agreement about period and style? A production schedule may not defuse every potential disaster, but it will go a long way towards achieving that end. Well before rehearsals begin, create and hand out to the cast a calendar that includes not only every rehearsal, but also every technical deadline. An example follows, with boldface print indicating rehearsals after regular school hours:

The calendar on the next page assumes a four-week production schedule, which is, of course, never enough time to do justice to a play. Six weeks would be far better; in at least one respect we do try to give students that much time. We usually read the play aloud in English classes two to three weeks before our rehearsals begin. We first try to clearly establish what is happening, scene by scene; we draw diagrams representing main story line and possible subplots, noting shifts of setting or time; we identify who the characters are, what their relationships are to one another, how they change. As we reread the script, students begin to probe characters' motivations, imagine how they walk, what their childhoods were like, and hazard guesses as to what their deepest secrets are. Students retell or enact scenes in their own words. Through it all, we try to build up a vision of the play as a world full of coherence and purposeful direction.

Sun	Mon	Tue	Wed	Thu	Fri	Sat
	Week one: Rehearsals begin		Props list due	Sound effects plan due	Sketches for costumes, sets, make-up posters due **Evening Rehearsal 7-10 PM**	Tech. reh. build platforms, flats, hang lights; begin costume work, work on sound effects
	Week two: OFF BOOK no scripts allowed on stage Music ideas due; props collected	Write letter describing reserved ticket procedure	Final poster design due; lighting scheme complete **Evening Rehearsal 7-10 pm**	Dance choreography due; check makeup box; distribute ticket letter	Posters up; work on dance with music **Evening Rehearsal 7-10 pm**	Tech. reh. finish flats; lighting and sound effects check; continue costume work; paint sets
	Week three: Backstage props list posted; prompting and lighting script complete	Makeup needs list complete; begin designing program	**Evening Rehearsal Semi-dress 7-10 pm**	Secure ticket takers for performances; check with maintenance about chairs	**Evening Rehearsal Semi-dress 7-10 pm** with lights, sound, and lights, set up chairs	Tech. reh. finish all detail work on costumes, finish painting; re-aim lights
	Week four: **Dress Rehearsal** First makeup call at 6:30 pm	**Daytime Performance** for school makeup call at noon	**Opening Night**	**Second Performance**	**Closing Performance** Bravo! Break down set and cleanup	

150

During these readings, casting ideas should already be simmering. Some directors allow students to audition for specific roles. The biggest danger to avoid is to have a student become fixated on one part before the casting is completed. The readings should, therefore, be fluid; girls can read boys' roles and vice-versa. Hearing as many voices as possible reading different parts may lead to a surprising casting choice. Ideally, the cast should be chosen at least a week, and preferably two, before rehearsals commence. With that much lead time, actors can at least become familiar with their lines and begin to imagine their characters into being.

Learning Lines

"Suit the action to the word, the word to the action."
(*Hamlet*, Act III, scene ii)

How can actors memorize lines so that the words do not become little corpses or leaden weights? The worst way I can think of is to simply repeat the lines over and over. Yes, some students can internalize their parts through such rote repetition, but they can also squeeze all the life out of their lines in the process. Unless actors learn lines in a dynamic and imaginative manner, they run the risk of speaking so mechanically that the director might have to resort to some extreme measures. A few years ago I worked with a gifted young fellow who had been cast in the role of Falstaff in *The Merry Wives of Windsor*. For some strange reason he had learned his lines in this barren, rote fashion, and his voice became very monotone and almost unintelligibly gravelly. I stumbled upon the notion of having him sing his lines in rehearsal. After some initial resistance, he warmed to the idea and began to sound like a silly Pavarotti belting out operatic phrases. I would not call the results musical, but the effect on his speaking voice was transformative. After just a day or two of this singing exercise, his voice acquired more mobility and vitality. He went on to become a Falstaff at once duplicitous and vulnerable, blustery and contrite, due in no small part to his remarkably improved vocal range.

Such emergency actions may not be necessary if the actors can learn their lines as animatedly as possible. Three approaches have proven effective for our actors:

1) Have the actors move when memorizing lines. If young people can get their lines into their limbs, their delivery will be much more dynamic and their gestures much more natural.

2) Have actors memorize lines using a closed-eye method. If they can visualize as vividly as possible what the character looks like—stance, gesture, facial expression, surrounding atmosphere—their speeches will acquire a vitality that can come from imagining such moments into being.

3) Advise students to use the memory-enhancing benefits of sleep to learn their parts. If they read portions of their parts each night just before dropping off to sleep, the mysterious, benevolent forces that work on them at night will help students internalize their lines in the deepest possible way.

Of course, for any of these methods to really work, the actors must first understand what they are saying. I cannot count the number of times, deep into a production, when a student would deliver some line blandly or unconvincingly. Several years ago a young man playing Don Pedro in *Much Ado About Nothing* addressed the following line to Benedick:

> Thou wast ever an obstinate heretic
> in the despite of beauty,
> > (Act I, scene i)

as if he were speaking Martian. I asked the student, "Do you know what that line means?"

"Not really," was his standard reply.

"Do you think it would help your character sound more insightful and authoritative if you did understand what you were saying at this critical juncture of the play?"

"Dunno. Probably wouldn't be a bad idea," the actor graciously acknowledged.

So, with the infinite patience and deep understanding of the adolescent psyche that every director of young people needs, I gently and good-naturedly explained what I thought the line meant. Whereupon, he retorted, "You don't have to scream! I'm not an idiot, you know." This lofty exchange was just one of many that demonstrate how rewarding directing can be. In any case, actors need to understand the words they speak if they are going to invest them with the meaning and conviction they deserve.

Chapter XV

Tangling Tongues to Strengthen Speech
(Repeat three times rapidly.)

During a production, we work on speech every day, usually as the first activity in a rehearsal. Most of us don't think too often about our speech, especially about the difference between consonants and vowels, even though they are the two building blocks that comprise virtually every word we speak. What is the distinction? Vowels are borne on the breath; all we need to do to speak a vowel is to breathe, vocalize the sound, and alter the shape of our lips and mouth slightly. The gesture is similar to the movement of calm and quiet waters flowing through narrower or wider channels in a riverbed. By contrast, most consonants are formed through friction. The breath encounters some obstacle, some resistance in the throat or mouth— like the roar of whitewater plunging over boulders down a canyon chute. The sound may be formed by closing the throat (to form the guttural "g" or "ng" or the unvoiced "k" or "ch"), by creating the friction of tongue against palate ("l," "t," "d," "n"), by compressing the air as it flows through the teeth ("sh," "f," "s"), or by impeding the breath as it passes through the lips ("b," "p," "m").

Except for "w" and "h," which are more akin to vowels since they are formed without such resistance, consonants require much more effort to produce. Of course, we are normally unaware of this exertion, but speech exercises certainly raise our awareness of the energy needed to shape our speech. Consonants require us to be "sculptors," to carve and shape the very breath we expel, yet many young people today show evidence of damaged wills through their manner of speech.

Two general tendencies in our students' speech patterns have emerged in the past few years. Either they speak somewhat metallically and mechanically, with clipped and almost robotic phrasing, due perhaps, in some part, to the influence of the video voices they have heard since early childhood. Or they mumble and slur their speech instead of making the effort to articulate—early Marlo Brando imitations, but without the expressiveness; such students are vowel-heavy and consonant-weak. Their speech lacks crispness and clarity; they deliver lines that sound trapped within them.

Much of the speech work we do with students is remedial in this respect. For the mechanical speakers, we try to get the sound out of their heads, to deepen their breathing and warm up their speech. For the languid speakers, we work to lift their speech out of their bodies, to encourage distinctness and vitality. In either case, tongue twisters emphasizing different combinations of vowels and consonants can be enormously helpful in enlivening young actors' speech. For example, a clipped and metallic delivery can be aided by lines full of round, warm vowels.

Old oily Ollie oils old oily autos.

Going to Cologne in a canoe
I met a curious kind of creature.
"Who are you? Some kind of kangaroo?"
"Oh, no, no, no.
A monkey munching mangoes in a zoo
looks more like you."

Ah! A marvelous mosque with woven walls
in the land of Allah calls to all.

These lines will have the most impact if they are spoken breathily, with the exhalation beginning from the diaphragm. To enhance fluency in these same young actors who speak as if they are intermittently spitting bullets, the following might help:

Lovely lady leading.
Lipping light laughter.
Lumbering loiterer laggardly lurch.

We employ the related exercise below especially when we are working on a comedy and need our actors to bring lightness and brightness to their normally ponderous speech:

It's a cinch
Which in me
Link-lock-who
Lock-lack-he
Flirting with
Wits here
Blabs

This little verse should be almost chanted lightly; students might think of speaking it as if tiptoeing over nails. It can even be stage whispered to great effect. The "who" and "he" at the end of the middle lines should be almost sung, sliding up to falsetto voice, in an accompanying vibrato.

Students with lazy, muddy delivery (and this includes the vast majority of today's young people) need to invigorate their speech, to bring will to their words. Dozens of tongue twisters emphasizing combinations of consonants can be employed to brighten and vitalize students' persistent mumbling.

B

> The big, gold-braided burglar grabbed a biodegradable dog.
>
> A box of biscuits, box of mixed biscuits, and a biscuit mixer.
>
> A big blue bucket of black and blue bruised blueberries.
>
> Three blue beads in a blue bladder rattle.

F

> Four fat friars frying flat fish.
>
> Ted threw Fred three free throws.
>
> A fat-thighed freak fries thick fish.

G

> Eight gray geese grazing gaily in Greece.
>
> Cows graze in groves on grass which grows in grooves in groves.

K or C

> Coffee from a proper copper coffee pot
>
> Chickens clucking, crickets chirping.

Creeping Greek grapes keep Greeks great.

Camp Glenbrook's glad campers grab blenders.

M

Men munch much mush.
Women munch much mush.
Many men and women munch much mush.

Aluminum, linoleum.
Linoleum, aluminum.

N

Knit nine gnomes in nimbus mutely musing.

P

The peaceful pleading priest preaches peace.

A proper crop of poppies is a proper poppy crop.

Tom bought some fine prime pink popcorn
At the fine prime pink popcorn shop.

Please, Paul, pause for applause.
Pause for applause, Paul.

R

The rat ran by the river with a lump of raw liver.

Really weird rear wheels whirl randomly round the
    long rough lake.

Wild Ruth's wine red and royal white wet roof.

S

Sheep shouldn't sleep in a shack;
Sheep should sleep in a shed.

She sews shirts seriously;
She says she shall sew a sheet soon.

Does this shop stock short socks with shocking spots
for shortstops?

The seething sea ceaseth seething.

Shy Sarah saw six Swiss wristwatches and six ripped,
preshrunk shirts.

Strange strategic statistics.

Soldiers' shoulders shudder when shrill shells shriek.

Slapped slimy slush shivers slightly.

The old school scold sold the school coal scuttle.

T

Tim, the thin twin tinsmith, twists with Tim's slim twin
sister.

Two tiny painters pointed to a pint of ointment.

Tom threw Tim three thumbtacks.

Th

Thin sticks, silver thimbles, thick bricks.

Three sick thrushes sang thirty-six thrilling songs.

The sixth thick thistle Cecil saw was Cecil's sixth thick thistle.

I spied three shy thrushes; you spied three shy thrushes.

W

Which wristwatches are Swiss wristwatches?

Wind the red wire round the white reel.

All of the above tongue twisters should be spoken slowly and clearly at first. Obviously, adding repetitions and increasing speed will raise the level of difficulty. However, one of the wonders of these exercises is that our tongues seem to have some inexplicable capacity for absorbing and mastering them over time. The student who today mangles one of the shortest and most difficult of all tongue twisters—"Peggy Babcock" (skeptics should try repeating it five times without a stumble)—will usually, magically be able to speak it perfectly three days hence, even without practicing it outside of class.

Students may see mastering tongue twisters as an end in itself, but most of them also recognize soon enough that such daily exercises have further-reaching effects. This heightened sensitivity to speech helps to give young actors' characters richer textures and deeper dimensions. If someone is playing Malvolio in *Twelfth Night*, he learns that by overenunciating consonants in the most fastidious manner, he creates a foolish figure in love with the sound of his own voice. If an actress has tackled the challenging role of Dolly Levi in Wilder's *The Matchmaker*, she may find that by dissolving her "r's," and by bending and redirecting her vowels through her nasal passages to acquire a Brooklyn accent, she may begin to sound like a most convincing yenta.

In their everyday life as well, young people's speech becomes clearer, more robust, and more animated. They acquire more "colors in their palette" for expressing the nuances of their burgeoning thoughts and feelings. Behind all of the improved communication skills and enhanced dramatic possibilities, another unexpected transformation is taking place. It is well-known by now that crawling in the first year of life somehow years later makes reading much less of a struggle than it is for someone who never crawled. How mysterious that some kinetic activity we perform as infants actually develops a certain readiness for reading later on.

The Greeks also understood this seemingly obscure connection between one activity and another. In our sports-minded culture, much attention has been given to the Greeks' love of athletics and to their founding of the Olympics. In particular, the ancient pentathlon has been hailed as the prototype of the modern decathlon, the defining event in any Olympics. Yet few people know that the Greeks used the pentathlon events—running, jumping, wrestling, discus, and javelin throwing—as a training for the development of cognitive and dramatic skills. Was it an accident that Plato was a champion wrestler in his youth? Or did all that wrestling training prepare him to grapple with deep philosophical riddles?

Another event—javelin throwing—aided speech formation. As far-fetched as this may seem, consider that both activities involve a "reaching back"; in the case of speaking, we had better gather our thoughts before verbalizing them. Both activities then require a taking aim at a target before letting fly. Even our vocabulary retains the faintest hint of the relationship between these two tasks. The javelin hurler's delivery must be straight and true. The effective speaker's delivery must be the same if he or she is to hit the mark. For the Greeks, then, the effect of such physical movement went far beyond mere athletic excellence.

In a similar fashion, speech work may also have an unexplainable, salutary effect on another part of our being—it strengthens forces of individuality in each of us. Perhaps this is not very surprising when one thinks of the uniqueness of every human voice. Is it not a source of wonderment that every voice in the world has its own distinctive timbre? The particular inflection and pitch of a friend's voice can identify that person as accurately as fingerprints. If we strive to refine our speech, is it so far-fetched to think that such efforts work deeply on the very source of our individuality, fortifying and quickening that sense of self we call our ego? Teachers, then, whose task it is to guide young people into a healthy sense of themselves, can further this end through concerted speech work with their students. In this larger context, every tongue twister, every exercise we offer them, builds ego forces for the distant future.

It should be mentioned here that Rudolf Steiner also used archetypal gestures to enhance speech and drama work. He identified six basic qualities of speech and accompanying gestures that reflect people's varying relationships to the world around them. They are briefly summarized below:

> 1. Quality: **indicating**, directing, pointing out
> Gesture: pointing
> Voice: sharp, incisive in tone. "Please do it."

This pointing gesture can be in the nature of a command, but it can also draw our attention to some external truth. "There it is." The famous speech from Christopher Fry's *A Sleep of Prisoners* serves as a resounding illustration:

The human heart can go to the lengths of God.
Dark and cold we may be, but this
Is no winter now. The frozen misery
Of centuries breaks, cracks, begins to move,
The thunder is the thunder of the floes,
The thaw, the flood, the upstart spring.
Thank God our time is now when wrong
Comes up to face us everywhere,
Never to leave us till we take
The longest stride of soul men ever took.
Affairs are now soul size.
The enterprise
Is exploration into God.
Where are you making for?
It takes
So many thousand years to wake,
But will you wake for pity's sake?
                         (p. 209)

   2. Quality: **thoughtful**, reflective, pondering
      Gesture: holding onto oneself
       Voice: longer, drawn-out speech, even ponder-
       ous

This gesture should reinforce the impression of an inner activity, a ruminating or musing. Holding one's fingers pressed against the temple or brow or chin is a fairly typical way to indicate such reflectiveness. Any number of speeches in *Hamlet* convey this quality, but none more stirringly than the "To be or not to be" soliloquy:

         . . . To die—to sleep.
To sleep—perchance to dream: Ay, there's the rub!
For in that sleep of death what dreams may come
When we have shuffled off this mortal coil,
Must give us pause. There's the respect

That makes calamity of so long life,
For who would bear the whips and scorns of time,
The oppressor's wrong, the proud man's contumely,
The pangs of despised love, the law's delay,
The insolences of office, and the spurns
That patient merit of the unworthy takes,
When he himself might his quietus make
With a bare bodkin? Who would these fardels bear,
To grunt and sweat under a weary life,
But that the dread of something after death
The undiscovered country, from whose bourn
No traveler returns—puzzles the will,
And makes us rather bear those ills we have
Than fly to others that we know not of?
Thus conscience does make cowards of us all . . .

(*Hamlet*, Act III, scene i)

    3. Quality: **questioning**, searching uncertainly,
       "Can I do this?"
      Gesture: arms and hands groping forward
      Voice: tremulous, faltering, hesitant

The direction here is outward instead of inward, but obstacles appear which challenge the individual and leave the achievement of some objective in doubt. After he agrees to murder the king, Macbeth's agitated conscience leads him to the following moment:

Is this a dagger which I see before me,
The handle toward my hand? Come, let me clutch thee!
I have thee not, and yet I see thee still.
Art thou not, fatal vision, sensible
To feeling as to sight? or art thou but
A dagger of the mind, a false creation
Proceeding from the heat-oppressed brain?

(*Macbeth*, Act II, Scene i)

4. Quality: **antipathy**. "I'm busy. You're insignificant. Get out!"
   Gesture: hand(s)/arm(s) thrusting away from the body
   Voice: hard, cold, consonantal

This gesture is unambiguously sharp and dismissive. Both gesture and speech have a hard edge. Another speech from *A Sleep of Prisoners* captures the quality of this gesture effectively:

Any damn where he makes himself at home.
The world blows up, there's Pete there in the festering
bomb-hole making cups of tea. I've had it
Week after week till I'm sick.

(p. 164)

5. Quality: **sympathy,** affirmation, comfort
   Gesture: reaching out, as if to touch
   Voice: gentle, soothing. "I'm here for you."

Both gesture and speech are full of warmth. The palms of the hands should feel as if they are radiating that warmth in the direction of the intended party. In *Cyrano de Bergerac's* classic balcony scene, written by Edmond Rostand, we can experience this mood almost viscerally:

. . . Can you feel
My soul, there in the darkness, breathe on you?
—Oh, but tonight, now, I dare say these things—
I . . . to you . . . and you hear them! . . . It is too much!
In my most sweet unreasonable dreams,
I have not hoped for this! Now let me die,
Having lived. It is my voice, mine, my own,
That makes you tremble there in the green gloom
Above me—for you do tremble, as a blossom

Among the leaves—You tremble, and I can feel,
All the way down along these jasmine branches,
Whether you will or no, the passion of you
Trembling . . .

(Act III, p. 110)

6. Quality: **withdrawing** into oneself. "I would
rather be alone."
Gesture: hands thrusting away from body
Voice: curt and clipped, but not hostile

This quality can be confused with antipathy if not properly understood. The intention here is to hold one's ground, to protect one's privacy, perhaps. The gesture lacks the sharp and cutting character of the antipathetic thrust. Rather, the hands push away slowly but firmly, as if to create some personal space. The lines below from T.S. Eliot's *Murder in the Cathedral* reflect this mood:

Then I leave you to your fate.
 I leave you to the pleasures of your vices
Which will have to be paid for at higher prices.
Farewell, my lord, I do not wait upon ceremony.
I leave as I came, forgetting all acrimony.
Hoping that your present gravity
Will find excuse for my humble levity.
If you will remember me, My lord, at your prayers,
I will remember you at kissing-time below the stairs.

(p. 25)

These qualities of speech and their accompanying gestures were not intended to represent the entire range of dramatic possibilities onstage. Rather, the gestures might serve as bodily experiences to help enliven actors' speech. We have occasionally incorporated them into warm-up exercises to help actors explore the gestures and intentions of their characters.

Once work on a production begins, two other exercises can be employed to counteract the tendency to speak too softly. Many young actors have the hardest time being heard onstage. Some will speak softly out of timidity, others out of obliviousness, still others out of a kind of lethargy. No matter how energetically the director exhorts his or her charges, certain students will simply not understand the need to project to the back of the hall.

Exercise 72: COUNTING TO TEN
One effective way to stretch both young actors' vocal chords and their awareness is to ask them to count to ten aloud. The only condition is that each number the actors speak is louder than the one before it. 1–2–3–4–5–6– and so on. Most students will begin too loudly and reach their maximum volume by 5 or 6. Others will hold back, afraid to let go with ear-piercing bellows on the high numbers. But with repeated attempts, young actors will develop a capacity for modulating the volume of their voices, so that the director might say, "Franny, you need to speak those lines at an "8" instead of a "3."

Exercise 73: HURLING THE JAVELIN
Ideally, to aid in their vocal work, students might have access to real javelins and an unpeopled field nearby where they can practice their deliveries. Since few schools have such equipment readily available, an imaginative exercise may be nearly as effective. Have students stand with plenty of room around them, in lines facing the back of the hall or auditorium in which they rehearse. Then ask them to create an imaginary javelin, to reach back as far as they can, and then to fling it through that back wall, turning their shoulders, shifting their weight from back to front foot. Simultaneously, have them speak some line with strong consonants—we use "Dart may these boats, through darkening gloaming"—hurling the javelin on "Dart," and then using the rest of the line to watch the flight of the spear as

it sails out of sight. This follow-through is critical to the exercise, because adolescents have a tendency to speak words the way carbonated bubbles burst on the surface of the seltzer water—once they're spoken, they pop and disappear. Young actors don't always experience the extension, the "flight" of their words. This javelin hurling can stretch their awareness, from the reaching back— which is akin to finding the idea behind the words—to the delivery and follow-through. As they witness the arc of the javelin, they can become more mindful of the arc and the impact of their words. Whether students hurl actual javelins or perform such an action using their imaginations, the exercise should sharpen their sense of intentionality when they deliver their lines.

Chapter XVI

Technical Tasks

A sleek new automobile rolls off the assembly line looking so seamlessly constructed that it requires a leap of imagination to picture the piecemeal, detailed labor of welding, bolting, and fitting glass, metal, fabric, and rubber parts together. Similarly, when the curtain goes up on a play, few in the audience without dramatic experience ever realize how much effort it takes to synthesize the work of costumers, set and lighting designers, musicians, carpenters, sound technicians, and makeup artists. Yet from the inception of a production, all these technical elements and more must be integrated into the grand vision of the play. The first essential step in mounting a production is to articulate that vision. Before scissors, hammer, or paintbrush can be employed, the director and his/her associates need to create a conception of the play that will channel everyone's efforts in the same artistic direction. What time period will best suit this particular Shakespeare play? I have seen Hamlet's ghost booted and helmeted as a Nazi soldier, Falstaff and the merry wives he pursues living in a mining town of the old west, midsummer night's lovers in modern dress wandering through Oberon's casino. Not all of these inventive motifs necessarily improved upon Shakespeare's original settings, but they nevertheless served as the unifying inspiration for the work onstage and off.

Once a course has been charted, technical crews need to be assembled. In most amateur theater, this usually means two very separate groups of specialists working on a production—actors on the one hand, and technical staff on the other, with the latter's unsung labors serving the more visible and celebrated efforts of the former. Over the years, however, we have settled on an approach that melds the two groups into one. In our play productions, the actors are the technicians; all of the technical crew members also act. In a recent show entitled *Museum*, the young man playing the lead spent dozens of extra hours constructing clothesline dummies out of chicken wire, Styrofoam, and latex. Other members of the cast built pedestals for the outlandish sculptures they created out of animal skeletons, shells, fur, and bits of metal. Still others hung lights, painted sets, composed music for a guard's "dance of protest," and transformed drab gray jackets into guards' costumes by sewing gold piping on the lapels, cuffs, and shoulders. Virtually every technical task, from the designing and drawing of the play poster to sweeping the hall after striking the set, was completed by the cast.

Certainly adolescents cannot be expected to tackle all the technical aspects of a play without guidance. The handwork, music, woodworking, and eurythmy teachers—even the handy maintenance supervisor—have helped to oversee student initiatives behind the scenes. Parents with theatrical or technical background have been invaluable resources; many have been exceedingly generous in volunteering their time. In recent productions, one parent, who made a living as a stuntman, taught the students the finer points of stage fighting for a scene in *The Grapes of Wrath*. Another took responsibility for the lavish costuming needs of *The Matchmaker*. It is imperative, however, that such volunteers understand the overall conception of the play, and that they are working with, and not instead of, the student/actors.

The advantages of having the cast assume responsibility for the technical aspects of a play far outweigh the drawbacks. Yes, it requires a greater time commitment from the actors, who might otherwise focus their attentions solely on the demands of their roles. They will probably not paint a backdrop or design a lighting scheme or play the cello as expertly as professionals might. However, they will have an experience of a theatrical production in its entirety, and they may appreciate how their offstage efforts served that totality. They may also feel the deep satisfaction of having used their hands as well as their minds, hearts, and voices to create the magical arena of a play.

As has been mentioned earlier, drama contains the potential for the best and worst of human aspirations. It can become the fire that warms bone-chilled travelers or, uncontrolled, it can consume a forest. At theater's worst, would-be actors strut onstage purely for the self-aggrandizing recognition and adulation; their every gesture seems to trumpet, "Pay tribute to my brilliance." Actors who do not have to concern themselves with any of the mundane technical aspects of a production are more likely to fall prey to this demon than others who highly value and contribute to the technical work. However, drama can also find its highest expression in young people who see their task as service-oriented. In their efforts onstage and off, they serve the greater vision of a play. They may even create that rare moment when they share their collective work so artistically that both actors and audience are bound together in a kind of inspired communion.

As with many such intense activities, the participants do not want the "high" to end. They desire the triumphs and insights gained from the experience to carry over into their daily lives. If the young people have internalized the lessons that a play can teach, they can, indeed, preserve the essence of their theatrical experience; they go forward enlarged and energized. However, the danger is that some actors may want the applause to continue; they find it difficult to resume the classes, chores, homework, and after-school job without the acclaim. The need to make a transition back to reality is one reason we strike the set the same night that the show closes. What took a month or more of deliberate planning and artistic execution comes down in an hour. The players remove the platforms and flats, destroy the props that cannot be reused, store the ones that can, hang up the costumes, stack the chairs, and vacuum the carpets. The breakdown always tempers the post production celebration a bit, but it also brings the company back to reality in a striking way. They realize, as they sit on the now-empty stage, that the experience they have created no longer exists on a physical plane; instead, it lives on as imperishably as the memories of the players and the audience.

A few thoughts about specific technical work

Costuming—A much-admired colleague of mine who teaches high school basketry and bookbinding also, on occasion, helps to costume plays. She always begins her work by creating with the students some striking visual representation of the play's primary theme,. For instance, she once used the gesture and colors of a volcano to reflect the passions of *A Winter's Tale*, which is set in the shadow of Mt. Etna in Sicily. She then drew in the relationships of the main characters, linking them with certain colors. This colleague worked from the premise that color is the language of the soul, as well as an extension of characters' inner landscape. She found color combinations that connected each character to others and also expressed some essential inner quality. For example, on the volcano drawing she created for *A Winter's Tale*, she denoted Leontes using his black moods and raging red outburst against his wife, contrasted with a more muted but noble burgundy to represent Hermione, a deep red edged with the gold that reflected her pure nature. Once the hues became apparent, the costuming itself took on a much clearer direction. Whatever the final lines or styles of the actors' attire, this process of artistically charting the color connections of the characters ensured that the costumes reinforced the larger vision of the play.

As a general rule, actors should rehearse in their costumes as early as possible. The fairy in *A Midsummer Night's Dream* who stomps around in clogs or hiking boots simply cannot experience or convey the airy movement necessary to the part. One of the more controversial pedagogical principles in our school is that clothing influences consciousness. Adolescents, of course, bristle at this declaration, believing that apparel has absolutely no bearing on their ability to concentrate in class. Whenever this argument arises, I remind them of those Halloweens that fall on a school day, when everyone comes to school costumed, buzzing with excitement, and hopelessly distracted in class. They remember who came dressed as Dracula, complete with blood-dripping fangs, or what color their classmate's belly dancing veil, was far better than the lesson pointing out the difference between Whitman's and Dickinson's poetic styles.

In the theater, the truth that clothing affects consciousness is never more evident than when actors don their costumes. Almost immediately the student who wears a judge's robes becomes more deliberate in her delivery, more judicious in her manner. The young fellow who claps on sword, breastplate, and helmet suddenly stands more upright, strides like a warrior, speaks more decisively. Even if the company only has access to a part of a costume during the middle stages of a production—a hat, a shawl, a vest, an apron—wearing such apparel will hasten the transformation from students into convincing characters.

One other guideline: A brilliant seamstress/designer who used to work at the Sadler Wells Theatre in England once told me that the most effective costumes were those that drew the least attention from the audience. In other words, if they become showpieces in their own right, if they overwhelm the actor or jar the audience, then the costumes are somehow inappropriate.

Lighting—Illuminating a play is rarely a simple matter of making scenes darker or lighter. Again, understanding the effect of color combinations is all-important. The lighting designer must know that a predominance of green gels turns stage action eerie, that blues cool the mood as much as reds and yellows warm it. Shadows onstage can be highly dramatic, but undesired shadows distract from the action. A lighting scheme cannot really be tackled until blocking is fairly well established, so that stage areas can be defined, lights can be aimed, and different gels tried. Another reason for getting actors onstage in costume as soon as possible is to determine how the lights affect the colors of the fabrics. Under a red light, for instance, a green dress will appear quite black, while a red blouse seems much redder. Allowing enough time to experiment with lighting effects will diminish stress and unwanted surprises later on.

Stage sets—It would be presumptuous to offer any specific guidelines about the construction of sets, since they can vary from a couple of chairs and a ladder, as suggested by Thornton Wilder for *Our Town*, to an elaborate, if scaled-down version of a seventeenth-century French opera house, as in Rostand's *Cyrano de Bergerac*. Nevertheless, a few general indications might be considered:

1) Whatever the crew builds—platforms or flats, thrones or pirate ships—bear in mind that less might be more. Shakespeare may have had the right idea by

suggesting the merest indication of scenery and backdrops. Instead of building a complicated, heavily panelled tavern interior for a scene in *The Merry Wives of Windsor*, why not use a couple of barrels for stools and a simply constructed, lightweight counter for the hostess to stand behind?

   2) Increasingly, we have moved away from the two-dimensionality of cut-outs and flats. Rather, we have discovered the possibilities offered by fabric. When we produced *A Winter's Tale*, we dyed and speckled muslin in volcanic browns and reds, then stretched the sheets from the ceiling to the walls in overlapping, angular slopes. The result was a backdrop much more textured and three-dimensional than any flats could be. Under the lights, the mottled color effects created a much more visually arresting background than some static, realistic rendering of Leontes' throne room. In fact, such archetypal sets can convey a timeless quality that also serve as effective backdrops for a range of scenes. Their versatility can eliminate one of the greatest headaches of amateur theater—the seemingly endless blackouts when one set is carted off and another dragged on.

   Fabric solved another dilemma in a recent production of *As You Like It*. For years we had laboriously constructed trees out of a plywood base, a wooden substructure, chicken wire scaffolding shaped to resemble trunk and branches, and countless strips of muslin dipped in a glue-water solution. The resulting trees represented an improvement over two-dimensional cutouts, but they were also time-consuming to build, very heavy, and cumbersome to move on- and offstage. They also posed storage problems after a play ended. For *As You Like It* we hit upon the idea of sewing long cylindrical tubes of muslin. We dyed and streaked them the color of bark; then, to maintain the trunk's shape, we inserted several circular plywood discs horizontally every two to three feet and secured by stapling them to the muslin. We drilled holes through the discs, knotted the bottom with nylon rope, and threaded the rope through the entire trunk. To complete the effect, for branches we pinned a few more dyed muslin strips at various diagonals from the upper trunk to the ceiling and covered them with gauzy green tulle. Then, using a pulley system attached to the ceiling, we could pull the trees up into the fly space as they folded like Chinese lanterns. When we needed an instant Forest of Arden, presto! The muslin tree trunks dropped in seconds to the stage, a triumph of low-tech, low-budget theater.

3) Because most stage sets need to be portable, we try to build lighter, rather than heavier. Constructing with two-by-threes, and even one-by-threes for ribbing, instead of two-by-fours, will not significantly weaken your platforms or staircases. Using screw guns and screws rather than hammer and nails also allows for a quicker breakdown and recycling of materials. At the same time, build sturdily and secure every set piece. Years ago, a valiant eighth-grader playing Cyrano entered through an up-center door into Raguneau's bakery. Somehow, the door swinging shut behind him dislodged the entire flat from its precarious wire fasteners hanging from the ceiling. The result was not unlike watching a slow-motion train wreck. The flat hesitated for a moment, seeming to savor its newfound emancipation, then slowly toppled on Cyrano's unsuspecting head. To his credit, a somewhat stunned Cyrano buckled at the knees, but did not fall. Because the flat was made of lightweight muslin, he was able to lift it off his head, held it poised at an awkward tilt above him for a moment, as if deciding whether to speak his lines while simultaneously supporting the set piece. Wisely, he let it drop to the floor and proceeded with the scene. However, he involuntarily glanced behind him every few seconds to see if any other backdrops were planning a sneak attack.

Properties—Props can either be a constant burden to memory-challenged actors or provide the concrete inspiration that ignites their characters. How many productions have we all seen where the messenger digs into his pocket to deliver a critically important letter, only to discover that he must hand over . . . air? I watched a scene in one of our plays (through the shaking fingers covering my horrified eyes) where one participant in a sword fight dueled under the rather extreme disadvantage of having forgotten his sword. To make matters worse (or better, depending upon the audience's sense of humor), the surrealistic contest proceeded for perhaps twenty seconds—with one combatant slashing and thrusting with his very real sword, the other sheepishly parrying with one feeble forefinger—before offstage cast members realized what was amiss; then, one quick-thinking lad grabbed the missing sword and lobbed it from the wings towards the unarmed actor, where it clanked onto the stage, a marvelous example of *deus ex machina* if ever there was one. By contrast, when we were producing *Under Milkwood*, I saw a simple tobacco pipe transform one young actress from a painfully self-conscious gypsy into a most convincing and seductive lady of the night.

Of course, one can choose to eliminate the onus of having to remember props by simply doing away with them. Imagination is the most potent ally an actor possesses. Invisible props made real by skilled actors can utterly captivate an audience. However, most young actors are not yet adept enough to make the invisible so visible, and, as has been stated, props can assist inexperienced performers in deepening their characters. If props are desirable, then a system needs to be devised to ensure that they find their way onstage in a timely fashion; this is where a stage manager can perform an invaluable service.

Stage manager—there is an old saying that "God couldn't be everywhere, so he made mothers." The same could apply to the theater. Directors are hardly gods, but an alert stage manager can act as an indispensable backstage surrogate. At this amateur theatrical level, the histrionics that occur in the wings can be more eventful than what is happening onstage. Props vanish into a black hole; a dreamy actor unwittingly sits down on and crushes a queen's poorly situated cardboard crown—an argument ensues between the irate queen and the hat-crusher, one that threatens to drown out the scene onstage; the lead, who is supposed to be confronting the villain thirty seconds from now, is outside the building chatting with a friend; the wrong sound effects tape is in, so instead of the sound of screeching brakes and a head-on collision, the audience hears a dramatic organ playing Bach's "Dorian Toccata and Fugue in D Minor for Organ."

If the director must be in the house, perhaps to fortify an unsure lighting operator, it will be the stage manager who deals with all the backstage crises. Such an individual must be well-organized, direct without being dictatorial, and most important, unflappable. Usually one or two students in a given cast can be quite successful in this capacity, but they must be content with cameo acting roles themselves.

Most potential disasters can be avoided with proper foresight. A well-ordered crate with all necessary props can be located just offstage. Lists of entrances and exits and prop reminders can be posted in the same area. The stage manager checks actors' costumes for hanging threads and open flies. She calms a classmate about to miss his first cue because he is hyperventilating from stage fright, then gives him a helpful shove into the scene. Such an effective stage manager can add years to a harried director's career.

Chapter XVII

A Sample Production Sequence

"The time is out of joint."
(*Hamlet*, Act I, scene v)

Suppose we had before us the daunting challenge of performing *As You Like It* three or four weeks hence. Our task will only be possible if we have already followed the suggestions above, that is, edited liberally, read and really understood the play in its entirety several weeks in advance, assigned parts, handed out production schedules, and begun to learn lines as imaginatively as possible.

Actors will need to recognize in the early stages of our readings that this play contains an archetypal polarity between the treachery and divisiveness of the court and the restorative powers of simple goodness and love flourishing in the Forest of Arden. Duke Fredrick rules the court with a Machiavellian grip; having overthrown and exiled his older brother Duke Senior, Frederick now banishes his brother's daughter Rosalind. Accompanied by her lifelong friend Celia, Frederick's own daughter, and by Touchstone the clown, she goes into the forest to find her father. The noble Orlando must also flee, for his life has been threatened by his envious brother Oliver. No one is safe in this insidious atmosphere.

By contrast, Duke Senior lives amid the tranquility and bounty provided by nature. He has come to recognize that

> Sweet are the uses of adversity,
> Which like the toad, ugly and venomous,
> Wears yet a precious jewel in his head;
> And this our life, exempt from public haunt,
> Finds tongues in trees, books in the running
>   brooks,
> Sermons in stones, and good in everything.
>   (Act II, scene i)

This setting provides another kind of enlightenment for the exodus of characters from the court. During the play Rosalind, Orlando, Celia, and perhaps most remarkably, Touchstone the clown all find their soulmates and pledge their undying troth. The Forest of Arden not only rewards the virtuous, it also transforms the misguidedly wicked. By the play's end, both Duke Frederick and Oliver have shed their "snakeskins." Oliver repudiates his evil ways after first being rescued from a lion by Orlando and then falling in love with Celia. Frederick meets a holy man in the forest, finds enlightenment, and promptly restores his brother to his rightful dukedom.

Clearly Shakespeare intended to emphasize this contrast between the corrupt court and the healing forest. With such a polarity, we can trace the progression from acting upon the baser impulses of our lower selves to the harmonizing, ennobling effects of living life guided by our higher selves. The playwright's message seems clear here; every aspect of the play—the sets, costumes, atmosphere onstage, and characters' interactions—must reinforce this movement from corruption to redemption, from divisiveness to reconciliation.

Week One—Exploring the Physical: Establishing the Where, Introducing the Who

Each of our daily rehearsals can be divided into three parts:

1) warm-ups and exercises,
2) class conversation focusing on tasks to be accomplished or on problems needing resolution,
3) actual rehearsal of individual scenes or run-throughs of larger segments of the play.

Hearkening back to the organic sequence we have successfully used over the past two decades, we might spend the first week familiarizing the cast with the physical space of the play—entrances and exits, general location of set pieces, and the first tentative movements of characters in relation to one another. Thus, the primary work of the first week's rehearsals would be to guide the cast through an initial blocking of the entire play, ideally an act per day. However, before embarking on this journey, cast members need to warm up, both vocally and bodily, and to begin character-building. Possible first week exercises and a few interesting blocking problems are described below:

Rehearsal 1: Tongue twisters loaded with crisp consonants , such as "Two tiny painters pointed to a pint of ointment," or "Creeping Greek grapes keep Greeks great" sharpen the actors' attention from the outset and also help them articulate more clearly than they normally speak. We might also PASS A SOUND (Exercise 6), or PASS A CLAP (Exercise 8), and then do CIRCLE MIRROR (Exercise 16).

Breaking out of the circle, students now begin to walk around the room, first over different terrains, with WAYS OF WALKING (Excrcise 28), or THE FOUR ELEMENTS (Exercise 27), then perhaps in character. Initial attempts to walk in character are often, unsurprisingly,

notoriously unsuccessful. Students either create carica-
tures, or they simply continue to walk as themselves. Two
exercises can help immensely, especially when used in tan-
dem. The first is the daily visualization of each actor's character, called CLOSED EYES (Exercise 31); as students begin imagining their characters into being, they will also start
to translate that imagination into their gestures and voices.
The other effective exercise is WALKING IN AND OUT
OF CHARACTER (Exercise 33), which helps students begin to feel the difference between their own gaits and their
characters'. Frequent switching from their normal walk to
their characters' will gradually sharpen the distinction between the two.

   After a good half-hour to forty minutes of warm-
ups and exercises, the cast sits down for an overview of
the production process. Technical tasks will have been assigned before now, so students can begin to organize themselves in various crews (see section on **Technical Tasks** for
amplification). We go over the production schedule, alert
the cast to upcoming deadlines, and address any thematic
issues informing our understanding of the play. One student asks why Rosalind seems to relish the role of
puppetmaster once she dons the disguise of Ganymede and
toys with Orlando in the forest. "Why doesn't she drop
the manly act once she knows Orlando is crazy about her
and reveal her true identity?" A lively discussion ensues
about the wooing game and the issue of power in relationships before we turn to blocking.

   In subsequent weeks, students will divide up to
work on scenes in different locations during the primary
rehearsal time. But as tedious as it can be for actors not
directly involved onstage, having everyone there for the
blocking phase helps to build a common vision of the play.
On our cramped stage, it will be critically important for
actors to see how far the stage-right court extends towards
and interpenetrates the area of the stage-left forest. During

this first week, actors will still have their scripts onstage, a necessary evil because students will need to note entrances, exits, crosses, and so on. However, scripts impede the acting process and get in the way of gesture and character interaction. The sooner scripts can be dispensed with, the better.

One major, initial Act I blocking challenge in *As You Like It* is the wrestling scene between Charles and Orlando. How can we stage it so that it seems somewhat plausible that the Goliath-like Charles can be knocked unconscious by the valiant but overmatched Orlando? We decide to exploit Charles' own muscle-bound bulk and hulking immobility; Orlando will leap upon his back and ride him until Charles dizzies from his clumsy turning and twisting to rid himself of this "leech." Then Orlando will use a feigned forearm shiver to deck the charging, reeling hulk. Thankfully, one of the actors has taken classes in some martial art or another and knows how to fall with such a thwack on the stage that it sounds as if he must have broken several bones when he lands. However, he invariably bounces up after every tumble and gladly teaches the technique to his theatrical adversary. The grappling must be rehearsed repeatedly, within a carefully prescribed area, so as not to injure either actor or the interested onlookers.

Rehearsal 2: More tongue twisters, such as "A proper crop of poppies is a proper poppy crop" or "Soldiers shoulders shudder when shrill shells shriek," can be followed by PASSING HOPS (Exercise 9) and PASSING A FACE (Exercise 5), as well as the BALL TOSS (Exercise 2). With the latter, have students toss a tennis ball or bean bag to someone across the circle, calling out the name of the intended target's character as they toss.

For movement exercises, students could play FOLLOW THE LEADER (Exercise 25) as a warm-up. Then they might pair up and engage in MIRRORS (Exercise 26), an activity that trains actors on many fundamental levels. They must become more observant, develop more self-control, and learn to speak and to listen with their limbs. After introducing STICK/BALL/VEIL/CANDLE (Exercise 29), the cast can begin to experiment with one or another quality as it might apply to the characters. The stiffness of the stick might be incorporated into an old man's or woman's gait, for instance, for Corin, the aged shepherd in *As You Like It*; the radiating warmth of the candle might translate into the noble, generous-hearted expansiveness in a character such as Orlando. After daily visualizing, the blocking continues for the remainder of the rehearsal.

A technical difficulty to be surmounted in the transition between Act I's court scenes and Act II's Forest of Arden is how to transform the set, that is, how to make the pillars and throne room of Frederick's court vanish and the trees of the forest appear in a matter of seconds instead of minutes. We come up with two fairly simple solutions; one is a painted forest backdrop that unrolls from a ceiling via a pulley arrangement and falls in front of the court set. But we aren't content with the two-dimensionality of the backdrop, so we also rig up "trees" made of fabric that can also drop from the ceiling and offer characters an obstacle to hide behind when necessary.

Rehearsal 3: Speech work might focus on "Four fat friars frying flat fish," or "Eight gray geese grazing gaily in Greece," or "A box of biscuits, a box of mixed biscuits, and a biscuit mixer." Circle activities could include PASS AN IMAGINARY OBJECT (Exercise 10) and lead into PLAYING WITH IMAGINARY PROPS (Exercise 32). Both of these exercises strengthen young actors' ability to make visible the invisible. At the same time, thinking about the props their characters might handle in the play helps the cast members deepen their understanding of their roles.

One direct application of this training with imaginary props occurs in Act III, when Touchstone and Audrey enter. As the clown in a heretofore pretty unfunny play, Touchstone needs to provide some immediate laughter with his entrance. Since one of his first lines is "I will fetch up your goats, Audrey . . ." we decide that he will come in tugging an imaginary rope behind him, as if he is pulling along Audrey's goats. The more he exerts himself, the more the offstage goats resist, until the rope breaks, and Touchstone goes flying backward, landing on his derriere. Watching the goats scamper off into the distance, Touchstone can now say with an odd mixture of contriteness and ardor,

> I will fetch up your goats, Audrey. And how, Audrey, am I the man yet? Doth my simple features content you?

Audrey, perhaps a bit miffed by her goats' escape, can reply with an air of superiority she surely does not deserve,

> Your features? Lord warrant us, what features?
> (Act III, scene iii)

Fortunately, the cast approves of the idea for the entrance.

Rehearsal 4: Following on the heels of the imaginary prop work, the speech activity might include HURLING THE JAVELIN (Exercise 73) to bring more a more emphatic, bodily energy to actors' lines. Another effective warm-up at this stage of a production is STATUES (Exercise 38), which encourages young actors to become more conscious of each other's bodily instruments and the physical space through which they move.

The Act IV blocking presents an interesting dilemma in scene i, where Rosalind-as-Ganymede encourages Orlando to woo her. The question has to do with Celia's positioning during the scene. If she is placed too far away, seemingly oblivious to Rosalind's manipulations, then it makes little sense when, after Orlando departs, Celia upbraids Rosalind by declaring that "You have simply misus'd our sex in your love-prate." (Act IV, scene i) So Celia must be close enough to hear Rosalind's misleading words without seeming to impose on the intimacy of the courting.

Rehearsal 5: Another essential and most helpful activity that might be employed late in the first week is Chekhov's CENTERS (Exercise 30). After numerous productions, students have praised this particular technique as a highly effective way of animating their characters through physical suggestions. Yet another stimulating activity is EXAGGERATED MIRRORS (exercise 37, p. 43), which invariably raises the energy level of all of the actors as they explore distorted versions of their characters.

The biggest blocking challenge of any Act V Shakespearean comedy is how to arrange all the characters who congregate on the stage for the final scene. In *As You Like It* this problem is complicated by the appearance of the goddess Hymen. Should she simply walk on, as Rosalind and Celia's escort? Should she descend from the heavens or appear in a flash of light or out of a thick mist? Should she move among the characters as she addresses them, which might humanize her somewhat, or should she stand above and separate from the assembly, presiding over the proceedings as a lofty divinity? Our answers to these questions will leave a lasting impression on the audience, so we need to decide how significant Hymen's role is in the play.

To sum up, the goal of the first week is to begin giving the production, again to quote Shakespeare, "a local habitation and a name." The speech work and circle activities, the closed eye, character-building exercises and the slow process of blocking all are designed to ground each scene and each character in some concrete, physical reality, while giving the cast a general sense of the play in its entirety. Once the initial blocking is completed and the scripts can be left offstage, the tempo and intensity of the rehearsals will quicken.

Week Two—Developing Character and Tempo

Rehearsal 6: For a comedy such as this, the almost nonsensical "It's a cinch," speech exercise helps foster the appropriate nimbleness and gusto in young actors' deliveries. They should learn to speak it lightly, as if they were tiptoeing over the sounds with their tongues, even at times in a stage whisper.

The acting exercises during this second week should take the cast beyond purely physical modes of expression. GETTING TO KNOW ME (Exercise 34) helps the actors make discoveries about their characters' inner lives. The more collaborative CHARACTER BIOGRAPHIES (Exercise 51) can further deepen the actors' understandings of the roles they are developing. What recognizable attributes of their current characters can be recognized in seed form when they were children? Was the melancholy Jacques, the sour little boy, always on the periphery of other children's games? Did the child Orlando possess even then the innate nobility that his older brother Oliver envied with such malice? Was Touchstone already the class clown? Was Phoebe already so proud? Was Rosalind already knowing, clever, and in control of most situations? Did she love to dress up as a boy?

As for actual rehearsal of the play, having an assistant director or colleague around at this juncture makes it possible to even consider mounting a production in such a squeezed time frame as three weeks. Most plays can be subdivided into scenes that enable different groups to rehearse simultaneously in different locations. After the togetherness of the first week's blocking, it makes little sense to work on a single scene at a time, with the rest of the cast merely spectating. With prudent planning, nearly everyone in the company can be occupied in concurrent scenes. For example, while the director is rehearsing the beginning of Act II, with Duke Senior extolling the virtues of nature to his lords, an assistant might be working with Act I, scene ii, which introduces Rosalind, Celia, Touchstone and Le Beau. At the same time, smaller groups can be rehearsing independently; Oliver and Charles can play their opening scene, while Orlando and faithful old Adam may work on the Act II scene wherein Adam proposes that they both flee the court. Jacques can be working on his "All the world's a stage" soliloquy, and the shepherds Corin and Sylvius may refine their dialogue about being in love. With double-casting, such simultaneous rehearsing can involve nearly the entire cast.

Rehearsal 7: Whatever speech work the cast undertakes during the rest of the week, have them use their characters' voices. Even the slightest alterations in pitch or inflection can immensely aid a young actor struggling to create a convincing portrayal. Touchstone may need to sharpen his articulation and quicken his normally ponderous speech; Jacques may be played by a girl, so she may need to lower the timbre of her voice; the country wench Audrey has to work on sounding dimmer; Duke Frederick, more imperious; Corin, more aged. Use the speech exercises to give the actors practice in perfecting their characters' voices.

As for warm-ups, ANIMAL QUALITIES (Exercise 36) may unlock new dimensions for some actors' characters. It may also be time to work more improvisationally for those actors beginning to latch onto comfortable but mechanical methods of expression. A conversation between pairs of actors in character, alternating between gibberish and English, might be a mild "loosener." Others might be ALTERNATING WORDS (Exercise 55) or FOUR-HEADED CHARACTER CONFESSIONAL (Exercise 56). Students might also begin working more consciously with their characters' personal tempo in exercises such as CHANG-ING SPEEDS (Exercise 39).

Rehearsal 8: Assume for a moment that a mini-crisis is brewing; for whatever reasons, several actors seem to be fearful about appearing foolish onstage. They are risking far too little, holding back in their character portrayals. They are either speaking too timidly or moving inexpressively. What can a director do? COUNT TO TEN (Exercise 72) during the speech work can be invaluable. Such restrained and tentative souls sometimes need to experience the liberating effect of wild exaggeration. IT'S TUESDAY! (Exercise 65) is a perfect activity to stimulate more risk-taking. Yet another helpful exercise for young actors having trouble with gesture ("What do I do with my hands? They feel like dead fish!") is to employ DUBBING (Exercise 57). Often students feel weighed down by their lines; having someone else speak them can help such people concentrate on gesturing more freely.

Rehearsal 9: To continue preparing the cast for enriching improvisational work, the simple but challenging circle game SLAP SNAP (Exercise 61) both awakens and energizes the entire company. Students may be ready for exercises that demand that they work together improvisationally but in character. STATUES INTO SCENES (Exercise 52) serves this purpose, as might some version of RHYMING DIALOGUE (Exercise 70).

In the scene rehearsals, a new difficulty arises. The boy playing Oliver and the girl playing Celia are supposed to fall in love onstage, but the boy can barely stand to be in the same room with the girl, much less look adoringly at her. At the moment he refuses to take her hand in the final scene. Where is Puck's "love juice" when we need it? It takes a long private conversation convincing the fellow that acting often involves putting aside one's personal feelings for the sake of one's character. He says simply that he cannot look the girl in the eyes without wanting to strangle her. I suggest that he look not at her eyes but at a spot somewhere above her eyes on her forehead. After much coaxing, he agrees not only to try this higher gaze, but to also take Celia by the hand in the play's final scene. Unfortunately, he never gets beyond holding it as if it were a dog's paw; this union between Celia and Oliver seems doomed before the echo of their vows dies away.

Rehearsal 10: Timing becomes ever more important in rehearsals. One effective sequence to employ is a version of the FOUR-PHASE IMPROV (Exercise 40), wherein groups of actors improvise—in character—scenes related to the play. All the betrothed couples might stage a wedding feast scene after the end of the actual play. Dukes Frederick and Senior might improvise the banishment scene that occurs before the play begins; Sylvius and Phebe or Audrey and William could improvise the first time they ever met. The aim here is to play not only with the imaginative interactions but with tempo. Have the actors play their scenes deliberately too slowly, then too quickly, before they find the most effective pace.

By the end of the second week, actors should feel increasingly comfortable in and familiar with their characters, able to identify their characters' deepest fears, greatest strengths, secret dreams, or some nagging physical ailments. They should have discovered some of the inner rhythms guiding their characters' lives—the tempo of their walking, breathing, speaking. The skeletal blocking of the first week will have acquired more clarity and certainty, especially if props and set pieces have found their way onstage. However, the interactions between characters probably lack convincing connectedness, and the stage spaces those characters inhabit still need another enlivening dimension.

Week Three—Adding Atmosphere, Deepening Relationships

The work of the third week focuses on invisibilities—the mood that colors a scene, the motives that impel characters to act, the feelings behind the pauses that heighten accelerations of impassioned dialogue. This is a critical phase of any production; can young actors reach beyond themselves and begin to charge the very atmosphere through which they move? Can they develop that most undervalued capacity—both in the theater and in life—concentrated listening? The tendency of so many actors is to listen only for the cue lines supplied by their fellow actors. Yet such acting rarely conveys believable intensity or intimacy between characters. That is why directors need to help young actors stretch their imaginations beyond their typically narrow horizons.

Rehearsal 11: Assume that for this production, the actors are still struggling to create the dramatically different moods between the court and the forest. The director can lead the cast through a series of exercises designed to elicit "atmospheric effects," beginning with WEATHER EXTREMES (Exercise 42). Then the actors need to experience EMOTIONAL ATMOSPHERES (Exercise 43), especially the diametrically opposed feelings of suspicion and trust, treachery and loyalty, uncertainty and security. In rehearsals, these atmospheres need to pervade every scene, so that the air onstage is permeated with a mood as palpable as the humidity of a tropical forest or the dust of a sandstorm.

Rehearsal 12: As the actors become more adept at imbuing each scene with its own distinctive mood, they can also begin to explore the potentially absorbing encounters between characters who carry contrasting personal atmospheres onstage. Nowhere is this more apparent in *As You Like It* than in Act II, scene vii, when Duke Senior and his men are just sitting down to a festive meal in the forest.

Orlando lurches in, half-crazed for lack of food. He assails the banqueters at swordpoint, demanding food in the fiercest manner that a starving man can summon:

> Forbear, I say!
> He dies that touches any of this fruit
> Till I and my affairs are answered.

Yet instead of reacting in fear or with an equal measure of hostility, Duke Senior calmly defuses Orlando's seemingly implacable fury with his generosity.

> What would you have? Your gentleness
>   shall force
> More than your force move us to gentleness.
>   (Act II, scene vii)

Here we can clearly see the fascinating juxtaposition of two contrasting moods confronting one another. However, unless both the wise serenity and virtue of the Duke and his men are as well-developed as Orlando's frenzied desperation, the scene will not deliver all the impact it could. PERSONAL ATMOSPHERES (Exercise 45) helps young actors cultivate this capacity for enlarging and extending their characters' soul moods so that they suffuse the atmosphere of every scene. EMOTIONAL MIRRORS (Exercise 46) can also assist in this process.

Rehearsal 13: As performances near, young actors often need assistance broadening their focus. Some are only interested in how their particular characters are developing. Others begin to get stage fright days in advance and become stiff and clammy onstage. In either case, they lose any real sense of connection with their fellow actors. Several exercises can re-enliven this contact and empathy. One is a variation of CHARACTER RELAY (Exercise 71). At this late stage of a production, the director can shake up a lethargic, anxiety-ridden, or overly smug cast by having the players assume different parts during a rehearsal. The actor playing Rosalind exchanges roles with the fellow playing Orlando; Touchstone and Audrey, Jaques and William, Dukes Frederick and Senior, Phoebe and Silvius, Celia and Oliver; each trades parts with the other. Then, without benefit of script, they perform selected scenes, ad libbing to the best of their abilities. They usually know enough of their fellow actors' lines to do a passable, and often hilarious, imitation of the scene in question. The aim here is to stir the pot a bit—to ease some of the growing tension, and to expand actors' consciousness beyond their own roles.

Rehearsal 14: In addition to the regular run-through practice that a cast needs towards the end of the production process, it may also be helpful to stage a SPEED-THROUGH REHEARSAL (Exercise 41). The SPEED-THROUGH is particularly effective in helping young actors see the entirety of a play. By their very nature, most early rehearsals proceed in a piecemeal fashion. One must focus intensively on first one scene, then another, often out of chronological sequence. Inevitably, young actors will have little sense for the wholeness of the play until a run-through. The SPEED-THROUGH serves that function, and the accelerated pace demands a heightened sense of anticipation on the actors' part that can only strengthen their sense of the play's forward movement.

In these latter stages of rehearsals, the director is ideally tightening and refining every scene—adding stage business, eliminating wasted or ineffectual action. Every gesture, every step, and every sidelong glance should be purposeful without appearing too artificially orchestrated. For instance, in *As You Like It*, the scene where Touchstone the clown meets and recognizes the bumpkin William as a rival for Audrey's hand needs improvement. Touchstone

should become convincingly intimidating as he first inter-
rogates, then terrorizes William. The scene requires William to cringe and back-pedal before the suddenly
fiercesome clown. Up to this point, Touchstone has been
more jocund than ferocious, and William has been more
bemused than cowed. However, when Touchstone advances on William and is directed to deliver several crisp,
well-timed jabs to William's chest to accompany the following lines, the whole exchange begins to work.

(Italics below indicate my stage directions to the actor.)

> Therefore, clown, abandon, which is in the
> vulgar, leave (*poke*), the society, which in the
> boorish is, company (*poke*), of this female,
> which in the common is, woman (*jab*): which
> together is, abandon (*jab*) the society (*push*)
> of this female (*push*), or, clown, thou perishest
> (*shove*) . . .
>
> (Act V, scene i)

Nearly always, such refinements will arise most successfully out of staying true to the text. If actors and director can illuminate the intentions living beneath the words,
suitable actions will follow.

Rehearsal 15: An intriguing paradox arises towards the
end of a production. On the one hand, rehearsals of the
play itself need to be approached with the utmost earnest-
ness. The players cannot have so much fun that they fall
out of character or get distracted by the horseplay so typical of teenagers. On the other hand, we must contend with,
and even allow for, that ubiquitous adolescent energy and
agitation, particularly as the actors' anxiety about upcoming performances increases. The SPEED–THROUGH and
CHARACTER RELAY rehearsals described above certainly
help to channel that turbulence. Another such outlet is to

orchestrate a rehearsal in which the actors play their parts in a variety of accents or according to different motifs.

For example, every actor in Act I, scene i, might begin *As You Like It* speaking with a French or Spanish accent, followed by an ever-so-proper English or heavy German accent in scene ii. Celia, Rosalind, and the Duke might try the ensuing banishment scene, normally bristling with Frederick's hostility, in an Irish lilt or an Italian accent. If the actors have trouble replicating ethnic accents, they could be directed to sing their lines as an opera, to croon them as if they were Sinatra or Streisand, or to become rappers. Yet another option would be to have them play a scene as cowboys, monsters, spies, or as six-year-old versions of their characters. One of the most effective genres involves asking the cast to play a scene as if they were in a soap opera; the resulting melodramatic delivery of their lines often helps animate certain actors whose characters were too pale.

The goal of such an exercise is not great theater; on the contrary, subtlety and attention to detail will, in all likelihood, disappear, supplanted by an atmosphere bordering on the burlesque. However, such a rehearsal will invariably relieve pressure through hilarity, and perhaps even encourage apprehensive cast members to enjoy themselves onstage.

Week Four—Giving Notes, Final Touches

The last few days before performances are never restful, but they need not be characterized by cold sweats or rising panic. Most rehearsal time is given over to runthroughs, followed by the critically important process of giving actors notes, that is, specific directions to fine tune lines, gestures, entrances, and so on. The director can give notes either individually to actors or collectively, our preferred method. Even though the cast is often weary after a run-through, we have found it more effective over the years to give notes immediately after a rehearsal, so the actors can 1) practice, or at least visualize, the alterations while the scene is still fresh, and 2) sleep on the suggestions. It goes without saying that the director needs to share as many encouraging remarks as critical ones.

One final recommendation in preparing for upcoming performances is a closed eye, HORIZONTAL RE-HEARSAL (Exercise 74). Usually the day before, or the morning of, our opening show, we find some comfortable, quiet room, carpeted if possible, and ask the company to lie down as if they were spokes in a wheel, with their heads toward the center. The actors then go through the entire play with their eyes closed. As they speak their lines aloud, they visualize every entrance, every nuance, every mood change. They need not put all their energy into blasting their lines in this run-through. Rather, they should concentrate on imagining every element of the play as vitally as possible. This experience of the play can provide the cast with a final, shared vision. For a number of weeks they have been building a vessel, but from many different angles—some have been planking the prow, others the stern, still others have been carving the figurehead or securing the mast. This exercise allows them to inwardly climb aboard, set their course, and begin sailing together

Thus, all of our efforts to work dramatically with teenagers begin and end with the cultivation of imagination, not as some whimsical flight of fantasy, not even as a means of creating theatrical truth. In some circles, imagination is accorded little respect; it is dismissed as either the trifling source of children's make-believe fancies or, worse yet, a misleading mode of perception, whose clouded filter distorts reality. We have become convinced over the years that working with imagination in the ways described here does not constitute an escape from reality; rather, it can plumb a deeper reality, one grounded in the material world but stretching towards, and sometimes even touching, a higher realm.

Young people need to exercise this incipient power of imagination, in part, of course, because it can help them become better actors. More significantly, however, imagination rightly nurtured can also become a vehicle for apprehending greater truths, in oneself and in the world. Like Walt Whitman, we can recognize that we are all larger than we ever thought possible, that we do, indeed, "contain multitudes." Through imagination as well, perhaps we can begin, like Wordsworth "to see into the life of things." In fact, in *Romanticism Comes of Age*, Owen Barfield reminds us that imagination can even bridge the gap between the self and the world. "Imagination is not content with merely looking on at the world. It seeks to sink itself entirely in the thing perceived . . . to overcome the duality between subjective and objective." (p. 39) Barfield ascribes to imagination the potential to actually span the rift that has led to the isolation so characteristic of our time. "It involves a certain disappearance of the sense of 'I' and 'Not I.' It stands before the object and feels 'I am that.'" (p. 30)

Seen in this light, imagination can actually become an instrument for addressing some of the rampant social ills that afflict our modern world—the loss of community, the growing sense of meaninglessness and despair, the dehumanization of the human being, the rising tide of violence. Someone once said that "Resorting to violence is a failure of imagination." On many occasions, Rudolf Steiner spoke of the healing power of art in general, and of imagination specifically, not simply as a remedy for lack of creativity, but as a means of elevating human interactions into a moral realm. The seeds for this moral imagination can be cultivated in young actors who work with a deeper purpose than merely staging a play. Drama can help them develop the empathy to identify with the struggles and strivings of others. Imagination can take young people even further; it can enable them to recognize the higher possibilities in others and to act—onstage and off—in accordance with that vision of the higher.

From The Skin of Our Teeth – *12th grade production*

Chapter XVIII

Plays That Have Worked

As mentioned earlier, finding suitable plays for young people is no easy task. Far too many playwrights of the past fifty years either have severely reduced their cast sizes or focused on pessimistic themes that dispirit instead of inspire. We have searched high and low for plays of substance that have some redeeming value as well as language worthy of students' consideration. The list below includes many of the productions we have staged (or have considered) over the past two decades. It includes male/female cast size, a very brief synopsis, and noteworthy challenges or possibilities.

Antigone by Sophocles (3 m, 3 f, and a chorus that was traditionally 15)

The third in the *Oedipus* trilogy, this archetypal tragedy revolves around Antigone's decision to bury her brother's corpse despite a decree by King Creon forbidding it. Sentenced to a living entombment, she kills herself, as does her betrothed, Creon's son, when he finds her dead. Creon's wife also stabs herself when she hears of her son's fate. It explores the age-old conflict between personal conscience and societal law.

The major drawback here is the dearth of leading roles, but choral work can be particularly engaging for students, especially with emphasis on masks, speech work, and choreography.

One might also look at Jean Anouilh's modern adaptation, with 6 male and 4 female roles, but without a chorus.

The Bonds of Interest by Jacento Benevente (13 m, 6 f)

A Spanish farce, written at the turn of the last century but set in the early seventeenth century. Written in the commedia dell' arte tradition, it follows the manipulations of Crispin, posing as Leander's servant, who uses his wiles to outfox the Pantalone and Dottore and arranges for Silvia to fall in love with Leander.

Camino Real by Tennessee Williams (27+ m, 12+ f)

This is Williams' grim yet poetic vision of life in some unidentified, Spanish-speaking police state, where ruthlessness, corruption, and cynicism seem to prevail over innocence, goodness, and idealism until the very end. A host of fascinating characters, from Lord Byron to Don Quixote, from gypsies to aristocrats, reside on the Camino Real, desperately trying to survive or, in some cases, escape. At stake is nothing less than retaining the core of human dignity.

Camino Real can be a stunningly theatrical piece, with a number of opportunities for music and creative choreography. The set requires two very different sections—the suggestion of tenements and dark alleyways on one side, and a faded but still luxurious hotel on the other, with a great flight of stairs bisecting the set that leads up to an upstage wall. Downstage, a dried-up central fountain needs to flow with very real water at the play's end.

Conference of the Birds from Farid U-Din Attar by Jean-Claude Carriere and Peter Brook (7 m, 6 f, but flexible)

A company of birds is in dire straits. Urged on by the Hoopoe, they go on a journey to find their king. They meet with both despair and triumph as they attempt to cross the seven valleys. Cryptic at times, profound at others, this can be a feast for the imaginative costumer and director.

The Crucible by Arthur Miller   (10 m, 10 f)

Miller's searing dramatization of the Salem witch trials echoes the U. S House of Representatives' Un-American Activities "witch hunt," which spun out of control in the early 1950s. A group of young girls in Puritan New England, flirting with forbidden activities, such as nocturnal dancing in the woods, escape punishment by blaming several townspeople of devil worship. Accusations fly, fear and superstition run amok, and John and Elizabeth Proctor become victims of the mass hysteria.

This is a grim, intense drama, with a number of juicy female roles, especially Abigail and Elizabeth. Costuming is relatively easy, and the sets can be very simple.

The Curious Savage by John Patrick   (5 m, 6 f)

Mrs. Savage has been committed by her children to a posh sanitarium in Massachusetts. With the help of the other colorful "guests," she outfoxes her relations as they attempt to wrest her estate from her.

This is light-hearted and farcial, anchored by memorable and zany characters. The set is an interior and requires parlor furniture, but offers few other difficulties.

Cyrano de Bergerac by Edmond Rostand (tr. Brian
        Hooker, or Anthony Burgess) (30+ m, 10+ w)

Cyrano de Bergerac is the classic story of a dashing, seventeenth-century swordsman with a poetic soul and a grotesquely long nose. He falls in love with Roxane, but she has eyes for another, the handsome but dull Christian. Cyrano helps Christian win Roxane's affections, but when Christian falls in battle, Cyrano resolves never to reveal that it was he who wrote the love letters that melted Roxane's heart.

This play has everything—an opportunity for elaborate costumes and sets, swordplay, beautiful language, unforgettable characters, and a story teeming with ideals of self-sacrifice, devotion, courage. It is, however, a long play; liberal editing would help. We eliminated the entire fourth act with a bit of fill-in narration.

Dandelion Wine by Ray Bradbury   (10 m, 8 f)

In yet another midwestern setting, a middle-aged man plagued by loneliness goes back in time as a stranger to befriend his teenage self.

We have not tackled this play yet, but it sounds intriguing.

The Diviners by James Leonard   (6 m, 5 f)

This absorbing, unusual tale tells of a backward young man who is befriended by a disaffected preacher in the Midwest during the 1930's. The boy's phobia about water and the preacher's efforts to get the young man to wash collide in a catastrophic climax.

As a backdrop to the relationship between the two principals, the play evokes the small-town feeling reminiscent of *Our Town*.

The Enchanted by Jean Giraudoux   (9 m, 11 f)

A young woman in a French village develops an obsession with the supernatural. A number of bureaucrats attempt to prevent her from upsetting the security and hidebound provincialism of their lives. They cannot, however, prevent her from falling in love.

This play has a charming, challenging female lead. Some interesting problems arise concerning how to present a ghost. Other characters are somewhat stereotypical or underdeveloped.

An Enemy of the People by Henrik Ibsen   (9 m, 2 f)

Ibsen's story concerns a Norwegian doctor who goes from hero to enemy when he learns that the town's main attraction—the municipal spa waters he first discovered—now have become a health hazard. No one wants to admit the truth of the doctor's findings, which would imperil the town's prosperity; the doctor, Stockman, cannot imagine compromising his principles.

Although the dialogue is heavy-handed at times, this is another sharply drawn dramatization of the conflict between public interest and private ideals.

Grandchild of Kings   Adapted by Harold Prince
    (23 m and f, flexible casting, doubling)
The play portrays Sean O'Casey's life. Narrated by the mature O'Casey, the play reenacts significant moments in the Irish playwright's formative years. The play teems with singing and dancing as well as funerals and family conflict. It celebrates the spirit of a people as well as the spirit of the playwright-to-be.

The Grapes of Wrath   adapted by Frank Galati
    (20+ m with doubling possibilities, 8-9 f)
John Steinbeck's poignant, gripping story chronicles the Joad family as they leave the Dust Bowl for the promise of a better life in California. Galati's brilliant adaptation is filled with humor, heartache, and ultimately, the nobility of the human spirit.

This play has a number of unique features, including wonderful possibilities for blues or bluegrass musical accompaniment. It also requires some ingenuity to create an old jalopy that is both mobile and sturdy enough to support several people.

Idiot's Delight   by Robert Sherwood   (17 m, 10 f)

In a northern Italian mountain resort during the 1930s, an international group of guests is detained because of impending war preparations. An American song-and-dance man and his show girls entertain, among others, a French arms dealer and his Russian paramour, British honeymooners, a German scientist, and several Italian soldiers.

The play provides another opportunity for live music, this time a small nightclub band playing show tunes from the '20s and '30s. The international cast also seems tailor-made for a variety of accents.

The Inspector General   by Nikolai Gogol   (20 m, 6 f)

This trenchant satire skewers the corrupt petty bureaucrats of nineteenth-century Russia. A clever drifter is mistaken for a government inspector and plied with bribes, propositions, and other blandishments by the townspeople, who get their just desserts when the scoundrel leaves just before the real inspector arrives.

It is possible to alter the script so that certain minor roles change from male to female, if the need arises.

The Italian Straw Hat by Eugene Labiche and Marc-Michel   (11 m, 6 f)

A potentially hilarious farce, this play is really one long chase, involving the misadventures of a young man about to be married, who leads the wedding party all over town to find a replacement for the straw hat his horse inadvertently eats.

Fast-paced, with lots of doors opening and slamming shut, this play proves that timing is everything!

J.B.   by Archibald MacLeish   (12 m, 9 f)

MacLeish's Pulitzer Prize-winning version of the story of Job is set in a circus arena. The language here is uncommonly majestic, and the quintessential questions posed—

about the nature of suffering and of evil, of the relationship between the human and divine world—elevate this play into rarefied realms.

The set need not be elaborate, but some central circle suggesting a circus ring demarcates the acting area. Two rather high platforms for Zuss and Nickles—MacLeish's vendors portraying God and Satan—need to be constructed. Masks for the divinities might add to the mystery surrounding those characters.

Jabberwock by Jerome Lawrence and Robert E. Lee
     (26 m, 17 f)

This play offers a light-hearted look at young Jamie Thurber's life, before he became the creator of the Walter Mitty stories. It is peopled by a delightful cast of wacky characters, especially the members of Thurber's family and neighborhood.

The set can be quite simple, except for the electric car that suddenly appears onstage. We used a disguised golf cart quite effectively.

The King Stag by Carlo Gozzi (tr. Carl Wildman)
     (19 m, 3 f)

This little-known, but charming story tells of a king who seeks a wife and the wicked minister who seeks to overthrow him. The play is really a fairy tale, complete with a magic bust and sorcerer trapped in a parrot's body, but it incorporates many of the commedia dell'arte characters.

The play requires a number of ingenious set and prop devices, including a parrot that flies, a bust that can laugh, two stags, and a sorcerer who seems to appear out of nowhere. The production may be best suited for younger adolescents.

Look Homeward, Angel by Ketti Frings   (10 m, 8 f)

This is a brilliant, Pulitzer Prize-winning adaptation of the novel by Thomas Wolfe, which depicts his coming-of-age years in the person of Eugene Gant, living with his turbulent family and an odd assortment of boarding house characters.

The play is filled with a compelling blend of humor and grief and features some memorable figures, especially Eugene's overbearing, materialistic-minded mother and his tragically flawed father. Both mother and father must be played by very strong actors, as must Eugene. One of the centerpieces of the production is a large sculpture of an angel, which can be a challenging artistic project.

A Man for All Seasons by Robert Bolt (11 m, 3-4 f)
Bolt brilliantly dramatizes Thomas More's struggle with Henry VIII and his minions to remain loyal to his sovereign without compromising his principles. All of the characters are exceedingly well-drawn, even the minor ones.

The set can be very simple. The only shortcoming here is too few female parts.

The Madwoman of Chaillot by Jean Giraudoux
(24 m, 15 f)
An often-performed production brings to the stage a colorful, daft older woman and her friends. Together they manage to derail a corporate scheme, which would destroy Paris in the process, aimed at extracting oil from the subsoil below the city.

The long-standing popularity of this play rests in the parade of charming Parisian characters, but the playwright's statement about human greed masquerading as "development" is perhaps more pertinent today than ever.

The Matchmaker by Thornton Wilder (9 m, 7 f)
One of the best American farces ever written follows the misadventures of two lowly clerks who work for the wealthy Horace Vandergelder. He is determined to find a wife, and they are determined to bamboozle their employer

by sneaking into New York to carouse. The matchmaker arranging Vandergelder's marriage manages to end up with Horace herself, and the clerks each find romance through a hilarious sequence of complications.

Dolly Levi, the matchmaker, must have real stage presence. The costumes can be glorious, especially some the hats, since one of the scenes takes place in a milliner's shop.

The Miracle Worker by William Gibson (7 m, 7-12 f)

This extraordinary story dramatizes the early relationship between Helen Keller and her teacher, Annie Sullivan. The play is funny, moving, and ultimately inspiring and provides a rare moment of genuine transcendence when Helen finally sees light shining in her lifelong darkness.

The members of Helen's family provide challenging roles, but the success of this production rests squarely on the shoulders of the two actors playing Helen and Annie. Helen, in particular, must be played by a girl with expressive body language.

The Mouse that Roared by Leonard Wibberley
(12 m, 16 f)

A microscopically small, bankrupt country in Europe decides to declare war on America, since history suggests that the quickest route to prosperity is to lose the war and then receive billions of dollars in aid from the United States. The plot of this satirical comedy about international diplomacy thickens, however, when Tully Bascomb and his band of bowmen win!

This is a fine ensemble piece, with a large number of substantial roles. Sets can be spare, but safety measures need to be taken when arrows fly.

Museum by Tina Howe (16+ m, 22 f, fewer with doubling)

A scathing portrait of the modern art world and its patrons, this play takes place in a modern art gallery, while a parade of intriguing characters react to the artwork.

The only significant shortcoming here is that little transformation takes place in any of the individuals in the play. The playwright focuses instead on the broader message established by her satirical tone. However, the array of fascinating characters makes this an absorbing, and often very funny, theatrical piece. The major challenge in mounting *Museum* is the creation of grotesque, contemporary sculptures and a rather elaborate clothesline complete with hanging dummies.

Nicholas Nickeby by adapted by Tim Kelly (15+ m, 15+ f)
    A decent adaptation of Dickens' tale follows Nicholas as he goes from the harsh conditions at Wackford Squeers' Dotheby Hall to Crummles' theatrical company to the Cheeryble Brothers' counting house. The language is sometimes pedestrian, and the play cannot possibly convey the scope of the novel, but the characters are suitably Dickensian and melodramatic.

The Night Thoreau Spent in Jail by Jerome Lawrence and Robert E. Lee (11 m, 6 f)
    This play arose out of the anti-war days of the Viet Nam conflict. It dramatizes Thoreau's brief stay in jail for refusing to pay taxes that would help finance the Mexican War. Through a series of flashbacks, the play explores Thoreau's early adulation of Emerson, his attempt to start a school, an ill-fated and fumbled romance, his handyman days, and his befriending of a fugitive slave.
    This intelligent script is laced with some of Thoreau's trenchant observations and a number of well-drawn supporting characters. The final scene is a challenging dream battle that requires heightened sound and lighting effects.

Once in a Lifetime by George Kaufman and Moss Hart
            (24 m, 14 f, doubling possible)
    This Hollywood comedy set in the 1920's chronicles the fortunes of three down-on-their-luck vaudeville

performers who parlay the invention of "talkies" into short-lived success. The production brims over with eccentric characters—film magnates, German directors, neglected screen writers, wacky secretaries, glamorous gold diggers, aspiring starlets, and, at the center, George, a slow-witted but good-hearted stooge who becomes Hollywood's most successful film maker.

This play is quite complex, requiring a number of different interiors and some "showpiece" costumes, but the breezy dialogue and vivid characters make this an appealing show.

Ondine by Jean Giraudoux   (15 m, 12 f)
Ondine weaves the enchanting but ill-fated story of a knight who falls in love with a water sprite. We have not tackled this piece in English, but an ambitious French teacher directed an abbreviated version in French.

Our Town by Thornton Wilder   (17 m, 7 f)
Wilder portrays universal truths in his loving depiction of a small New Hampshire town at the beginning of the twentieth century. His genius is to discover the extraordinary in the most ordinary, everyday lives of people such as George Gibbs and Emily Webb. The final act depicts existence in a spiritual dimension, and depicts the poignant relationship between the dead and the living. This is a classic of American theater.

Wilder has made this a remarkably easy play to stage, using only the simplest suggestion of set pieces—a few chairs and a ladder usually suffice.

Peer Gynt by Henrik Ibsen, adapted by Paul Green
(26 m, 12 f)
Ibsen's masterpiece depicts a wild, boastful, and irresponsible young man who tramples on others in his quest for self-gratification. During his adventures in foreign lands, he leaves behind one disaster after another, until he

finally confronts the button molder and the consequences of his egotism.

This is a play of epic proportions, of grand scope and vision. Its length alone presents staging challenges, and editing should be seriously considered. The hall of the troll king offers promising choreographing possibilities, as does the incorporation of Grieg's music. Peer is a huge role, so large that we divided it among three actors, one for each of the three acts.

Shakespeare

Shakespeare's plays are an annual staple of our drama productions and are familiar to most audiences, due in no small part to the recent spate of movie versions. As I mentioned earlier, Shakespeare's unparalleled language, unforgettable characters, and stirring themes make his plays a natural choice for directors working with teenagers. However, the chief drawback is the dearth of female roles. Some girls interested in challenging parts may have to content themselves with playing male characters. A list of our most successful Shakespeare productions follows:

As You Like It
A Comedy of Errors
The Merry Wives of Windsor
A Midsummer Night's Dream
Much Ado About Nothing
Romeo and Juliet
The Taming of the Shrew
The Tempest
Twelfth Night
Two Gentlemen from Verona
A Winter's Tale

Based on our experience with *A Winter's Tale*, the comedies and romances are more accessible for adolescents than the tragedies or histories. However, we would consider directing a *Hamlet* or *King Lear* or *Macbeth* if the right cast came along.

The Skin of Our Teeth by Thornton Wilder
(25 m, 11 f, doubling advisable)

Wilder's Pulitzer Prize-winning satire depicts the exploits of the Antrobus family through the ages. They battle Biblical plagues and the encroaching ice age in this wacky, anachronistic tale variously set in the New Jersey suburbs, Atlantic City, and a post-Armageddon environment. Through it all, Wilder's profound faith in humanity makes this play as moving as it is humorous.

The three related, but somewhat independent, acts make double or triple-casting feasible. A projection screen for slides is required, as are prehistoric animal costumes.

Temptation by Vaclav Havel   (8 m, 7 f)

Loosely based on the legend of Faust, this dark comedy by a contemporary playwright turned statesman gives the audience an experience of life in Eastern Europe before the iron curtain was lifted and the Wall came down.

Under Milkwood by Dylan Thomas
(29 m, 28 f, plenty of doubling)

Originally written for radio, the lyric richness of Thomas' script makes this a feast for language lovers as well as for theater aficionados. The play reveals the secret dreams and everyday activities of Welsh fishing village inhabitants from their predawn sleep to their private evening rituals. Thomas lovingly creates a world peopled with unforgettable common folk whose longings and griefs we recognize only too well as our own.

This extraordinary piece provides an opportunity for true ensemble work. There are no huge roles, only a palette of colorful characters who emblazon themselves in our hearts with very few actual lines. The interweaving of narration and dozens of vignettes makes it most challenging to stage seamlessly. Multiple staging areas and only the suggestion of a backdrop will certainly help.

Other plays we have not done but would consider:

The Bourgeois Gentleman by Moliere (8-12 m, 4-8 f)

Moliere takes a satirical look at the pretensions of people obsessed with status. It includes a number of parts that can be played very broadly, as the would-be gentleman is conned by charlatans and family members alike.

The Coarse Acting Show II by Michael Green et. al.
(variable casting)

These four one-acts parody *Moby Dick*, *The Cherry Orchard*, Shakespeare's Henry plays, and the avant garde genre. Monty Pythonesque in spirit, these pieces can be irreverent, sometimes in questionable taste, and very funny.

Dinner at 8 by George S. Kaufman and Edna Ferber
(14 m, 11 f)

On the outside, the setting is a posh dinner party for the upper crust. However, just under the surface, a seething cauldron of intrigue involving servants makes this play both humorous and moving.

The Good Doctor by Neil Simon (variable casting)

Simon has written a humorous series of vignettes based on several Chekhov pieces, including a sketch about a man who harangues a bank manager, another about a would-be seduction, and a third about a man offering to drown himself for three rubles.

The Lady's Not for Burning by Christopher Fry (8 m, 3 f)

A verse comedy portrays an enchanting woman accused of turning an old man into a dog. It follows the romantic entanglements of several men competing for the would-be witch's affections.

The Playboy of the Western World by J. M. Synge
(7 m, 5 f)

This lyrical story is set in an Irish pub where a young man shows up boasting he has just killed his abusive father. He is hailed as a hero, and two women vie for his hand, until the alleged corpse shows up.

State of Siege by Albert Camus   (24 m, 10 f)

The Plague, personified as a stereotypical dictator, and his female companion, Death, terrorize a Spanish city and attempt to strip away the inhabitants' essential humanity. Only the courage and love of a single man breaks the siege.

Street Scene by Elmer Rice (16 m, 11 f)

Rice's Pulitzer Prize-winning drama depicts life in a New York City neighborhood and contains some adult themes, including a sordid affair and a double murder. Now considered a classic, the play portrays the diversity of voices, the ferment, and the rhythms of urban life.

Thieves' Carnival by Jean Anouilh   (10 m, 5 f)

Larceny and romance intertwine in a faded resort town where an aristocratic couple and two attractive nieces encounter a trio of thieves. The younger pickpockets fall in love with the girls to complicate matters.

Tiger at the Gates by Jean Giraudoux (16 m, 7 f)

This twentieth century play updates the classic confrontation between the Greeks and Trojans described in Homer's *Iliad*. It focuses on Hector's disillusionment with the glorification of war and his decision to return the beautiful but soulless Helen.

The Time of Your Life by William Saroyan   (18 m, 7 f)
    Saroyan's Pulitzer prize-winning play focuses on a waterfront saloon frequented by vivid characters searching for happiness.

To Kill a Mockingbird adapted by Christopher S e r g e l , from the novel by Harper Lee (11 m, 9 f)
    This compassionate, stirring story, set in a small southern town, dramatizes one family's struggle to come to grips with prejudice.

Tonight at 8:30 by Noel Coward
    These nine one-act plays sparkle with Coward's characteristically clever repartee and showmanship.

Tonight We Improvise by Luigi Pirandello
        (approx. 50 characters)
    Pirandello's groundbreaking play is about a wife being courted by a man who finds her relatives quite daft. Improvisation, actors dropping out of character and directly addressing the audience, and mime are all techniques Pirandello incorporates into the staging.

You Can't Take It With You by George S. Kaufman
        and Moss Hart (12 m, 7 f)
    Kaufman and Hart offer audiences a humorous family portrait of a wacky family and friends, including a Russian wrestler, an ice delivery man invited eight years ago to stay for awhile, a grandfather who collects snakes, a hidebound business tycoon plagued by digestive problems, and, of course, young lovers.

        The best resources for finding plays are the catalogs from the Samuel French Publishing Company, The Dramatic Publishing Company, and Baker's Plays. Although dated, Theodore Shank's *Digest of 500 Plays* can also be helpful.

Index of Exercises

BIBLIOGRAPHY

1. Aristotle. *Poetics.* trans. Gerald Else. University of Michigan Press, 1967.
2. Barfield, Owen. *Romanticism Comes of Age.* Great Britain: Rudolf Steiner Press, 1966.
3. Brandreth, Gyles. *The Biggest Tongue Twister Book in the World.* New Jersey: Wings Books, 1992.
4. Boal, Augusto. *Games for Actors and Non-Actors.* New York: Routledge, 1992.
5. Bridgmont, Peter. *The Spear Thrower.* Ireland: An Grianan, 1983.
6. Brook, Peter. *The Empty Stage.* New York: Atheneum, 1987.
7. Chekhov, Michael. *To the Actor.* New York: Harper and Row, 1953.
8. Eliot, T. S. *Murder in the Cathedral.* New York: Harcourt, Brace and Co., 1935.
9. Fluegelman, Andrew, ed. *The New Games Book.* Garden City, New York: Headlands Press, 1976.
10. Fry, Christopher. *Three Plays.* New York: Oxford University Press, 1973.
11. Galati, Frank. *Grapes of Wrath.* Garden City, New York: The Fireside Theatre, 1990.
12. Gibson, William *The Miracle Worker.* New York: Samuel French Publishing Co., 2000.
13. Goethe, Johann Wolfgang von. *Faust.* trans. Walter Kaufman. Garden City, New York: Anchor Books, 1963.
14. Johnstone, Keith. *Impro.* New York: Theatre Arts Books, 1979.
15. Leonard, Charles. *Michael Chekhov's To the Director and Playwright.* New York: Limelight Editions, 1984.
16. Marowitz, Charles. *Stanislavsky and the Method.* New York: The Citadel Press, 1964.
17. Martin, Robert A., and Centola, Steven R. *The Theater Essays of Arthur Miller.* New York: Da Capo Press, 1978.
18. Rostand, Edmond. *Cyrano de Bergerac.* trans. Brian Hooker. New York: Bantam Books, 1951.
19. Shakespeare, William. *A Winter's Tale.* New York: Washington Square Press, Folger ed., 1998.

20. _____ *As You Like It*. New York: Washington Square Press, Folger ed., 1997.
21. _____ *King Lear*. New York: Washington Square Press, Folger ed., 1993.
22. _____ *Hamlet*. New York: Washington Square Press, Folger ed., 1958.
23. _____ *A Midsummer Night's Dream*. New York: Signet Classic, 1987.
24. _____ *Much Ado About Nothing*. New York: Washington Square Press, Folger ed., 1995.
25. _____ *Macbeth*. New York: Washington Square Press, Folger ed., 1992.
26. _____ *Twelfth Night*. New York: Washington Square Press, Folger ed., 1960.
27. Spolin, Viola. *Improvisation for the Theatre*. Northwestern University Press, 1999.
28. Steiner, Rudolf. *Speech and Drama*. London: Anthroposophical Publishing Company, 1959.
29. _____ *Education for Adolescence*. London: Anthroposophical Publishing Company, 1996.
30. _____ *Stages of Higher Knowledge*. London: Anthroposophical Publishing Company, 1990.
31. Thomas, Dylan. *Under Milkwood*. New York: New Directions, 1954.
32. Whitman, Walt. *Leaves of Grass*. New York: The Modern Library, 1950.
33. Wilder, Thornton. *Three Plays*. New York: Bantam Books, 1972.